Carlo Uccellini & Gemma (Ferrari) Uccellini

A Love Story and Their American Journey

Louis W. Uccellini

The Penny University Press
Floreant dendritae

Carlo Uccellini & Gemma (Ferrari) Uccellini
A Love Story and Their American Journey

Written by Louis W. Uccellini

Contributions by Dianne (Mulqueen) Sullivan, Nafra (Uccellini) Mulqueen, Lenard Mulqueen, Eugene Bellini, Louis D. Uccellini

Edited by Dianne (Mulqueen) Sullivan and Susan Uccellini

Production assistance by John Stremikis

Contact information: sluccellini@comcast.net

Digital photo restoration, content development and design: John Stremikis and The Penny University Press

First printing Mar. 18, 2014; Jun. 16, 2014; Aug. 15, 2014; Nov. 3, 2014; Sept. 27, 2016; Oct. 11, 2016

ISBN 9781492349839   ISBN-10: 1492349836

Manufactured in the United States of America

Lenard, Fred, Charles, Louis, Dianne, Walter, Robert, Sheila, Linda.

Picture taken late 1949.

Henry, Margaret, Olga, Jim, Emma, Fred Louis, Libby and Nafra.

Picture taken early to mid-1980's.

Linda, Walter, Tom, Dianne, Lenard, Henry, Robert and Fred.
Sitting: Nanny and Charles.

Picture taken August 1977.

Dedication

I dedicate this book to the Uccellini/Ferrari family: my grandparents (Carlo and Gemma), my parents (Louis D. and Margaret), Aunt Nafra and Uncle Jim, Uncle Fred and Aunt Emma, Aunt Olga and Uncle Henry, Aunt Libby and Uncle Clarence, all of whom provided the love and life's lessons that shaped the following generation. And to the second generation Uccellini's still with us: my brother (Thomas Uccellini) and cousins (Dianne Mulqueen Sullivan, Lenard Mulqueen, Frederick Uccellini, Linda Durr Chianese and Henry Von Thaden), and to those who are no longer with us to share in life's joy: cousins Sheila (Von Thaden) Picucci and Robert Uccellini, and my brothers Charles Uccellini and Walter Uccellini.

Preface

I grew up in Bethpage, Long Island, New York in the 1950's and 60's. My father was the first-born son to immigrant parents from Italy, my mother the oldest surviving child of a family of German descent. Growing up among a family of 4 boys and surrounded by many cousins, aunts and uncles living nearby, I often heard about my grandfather, Carlo Uccellini, who died when I was not quite a year old. I became a favorite of my Italian grandmother, Gemma (known to us all as Nanny), who was my only surviving grandparent on either side of the family by the time I was 4 years old. I heard the stories about my grandparents traveling to America from Italy on a crowded ship knowing they were never going back home to Italy. I heard about their hard work to sustain the family in the face of anti-Italian feelings that ran high in the late teens and early twenties and through the Depression in the 1930's. My curiosity grew. I wanted to know more about my Italian roots.

When exploring the connections between the current and past generations, the family genealogy, we all start working back in time from our parents to our grandparents and back through the generations. The usual goal is constructing a family tree. In doing so, we find that within that tree there are stories which emerge in every branch. And we find that the family history can have compelling stories that reveal the person behind the name and which shape the outcome of the current generation that we know as our life history. We find what historians already know; that the history of a family, a country, the World is shaped by stories of individuals.

The history of the United States has been shaped and enriched by the immigration of people from all over the World. The immigrant wave of Italians in the late 19th and early 20th centuries made history and provided a family-oriented culture and sturdy workforce that changed the face of the United States and enriched us all. As one explores the breadth of the Italian-American influence on the United States, we are again reminded that this history consists of compelling forces and circumstances that made people decide to leave their native lands, to travel to America and build their futures here. For each of these heroic, individual efforts there is a story that shapes the family, their home, the country; a story that reaches far beyond the actions of those individuals who made their journey to America.

This is one of those stories.

Louis W. Uccellini

October 11, 2013

Table of Contents:

Prologue

Try to imagine a smart headstrong man growing up near Parma, Italy in the late 1800s. After the turn of the century, his eyes look to America as the land of opportunity, a place to live a dignified existence. At the same time he pledges himself to a women he has known since childhood. He determines that his only hope to raise a family is to start this new phase of his life in America. In 1906, he crosses the Atlantic alone in steerage to set up a stake in this new country, in a place called Brooklyn, only to find out that the woman he loves is no longer interested. By early 1913 he learns that an elaborate ruse, perpetuated by this woman's sister, was the basis of his lost love. He is able to reestablish the link to his sweetheart and goes back to Italy in the autumn of 1913. He marries the only woman he has ever loved. He journeys back to America with his new wife and entire family, except for his adopted father, Giovanni Uccellini. He arrives in America on January 1, 1914 to begin his American life. ***This is Carlo Uccellini.***

Try to imagine a young woman growing up near Parma, Italy in the late 1800's, the oldest daughter of a family who owns a beautiful and productive farm called Cantalupo. She falls in love with a handsome, smart and headstrong man she has known since childhood, who has dreams of making it on his own and raising a family in America. She watches him leave in 1906 and then loses all contact with him. She is unaware that the break is because of her sister. She then rediscovers him in early 1913 through an incredible sequence of events. She pledges herself to him through a series of letters. He comes back to Italy, marries her and then takes her away from her entire family. She travels to America in steerage on a one-way ticket, arriving on January 1, 1914. She is the only member of her family to leave this perfect, idyllic farm, the vibrant loving family and her parents whom she has revered her entire life. She lives, works and raises five children in a foreign land, in an environment she barely understood and dedicates the rest of her life to her husband and family. ***This is Gemma Uccellini.***

Carlo and Gemma are my grandparents on my father's side. This is their story, a love story involving two very brave and determined people, the outcome of which provided the foundation for our family's existence. In the following pages I have attempted to tell their story based on my visits back to Italy between 1981 and 1996 and my conversations with Gemma's sister and two brothers. I also rely on my father's notes from his visit to Italy in the mid 1980s and the letters from Carlo to Gemma, written in 1913, that have miraculously been saved through the years. I have drawn from the recollections of my Aunt Nafra, close family friends Eugene Bellini and Perry DeLalio and cousin Dianne Mulqueen Sullivan to help describe my grandparents and their life in America. This is a complex story that includes birth names, the Catholic Church and family actions that could have completely derailed the union between Carlo and Gemma. Even now, I discover added details that lead me to correct dates and other accounts. Thus, changes or new sections may be necessary as others continue to fill in the details of this story, a task for future generations who owe their existence to Carlo and Gemma.

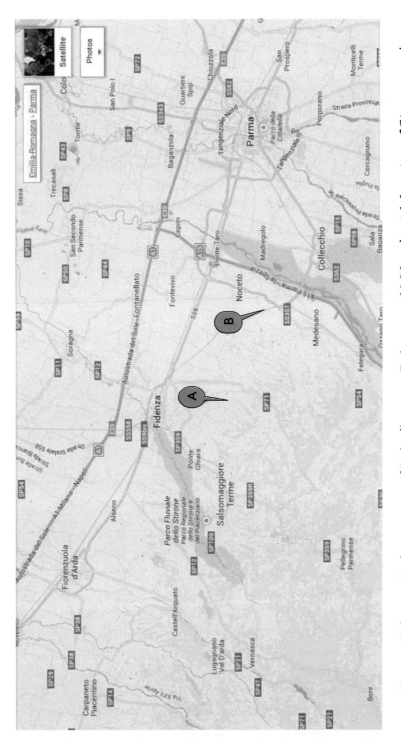

Parma, Fidenza, Medasano area of Italy, (between Bologna and Milano), with location of Siccomonte/ Cantalupo indicated by map pin "A" and the Villa Copelli indicated by map pin "B". North is on top of map, and East is toward right on map.

Carlo and Gemma: Story Summary

Carlo and Gemma's story begins near Medesano in north-central Italy southwest of Parma.

Carlo was born on July 6, 1883, in the "Villa Copelli" located outside of the city of Medesano, Italy. His natural born father was Luigi Copello, the son of the owner of the Villa. Carlo's mother, Maria Rastelli, was a house cleaner at the Villa Copelli. When Maria Rastelli became pregnant with Carlo, Luigi Copello admitted to being the father. Everyone recognized that Maria and Luigi could not marry because of the class distinctions. Instead, a gardener named Giovanni Uccellini, who also worked at the Villa Copelli and who knew Maria was pregnant with Luigi Copello's baby, married Maria and agreed to raise the baby as his own. Thus Carlo was born on July 6, 1883 and known as an Uccellini from birth.

Gemma Ferrari was born on January 17, 1886, the eldest child of Francesco Ferrari and Adele Bacchini Ferrari in a Ferrari "complex" located just outside of Medesano. Sometime between 1908 to 1911, the family moved onto a farm they called Cantalupo, a truly magical setting, located in the gentle valleys and hills in Siccomonte just west of Fidenza.

Carlo and Gemma knew each other as children playing together in their common neighborhood near Medesano. According to Gemma's sister, Anita, Carlo and Gemma fell in love sometime in 1902-1903 and pledged a faithful, lifelong commitment to each other. At the same time, Carlo developed a burning desire to leave Italy for America for reasons related to Carlo's drive to succeed and to leave Italy's caste system that treated landless people essentially as serfs. Carlo recognized that the nature of Italy's system, combined with other matters linked to the Catholic Church and the Copello's loss of the lands surrounding the villa, would pose serious obstacles to any attempt on his part to rise up within the Italian system.

Carlo's dream of living in America, to make his riches as an inventor and a farmer working his own land, and his desire for Gemma to be his wife came to a dramatic and nearly catastrophic clash, engineered in part, by Anita. Carlo, separated from Gemma by his first voyage to America in 1906, thought he had lost Gemma forever. Gemma thought all was lost with Carlo after his letters stopped coming from America. It was not until late 1912 or early 1913 that both Gemma and Carlo found out rather miraculously that Anita had duped them both into believing each other had moved on to others.

In 1913 they discovered that they were both still available and still in love. They recommitted to marrying to each other. Carlo returned to Italy and married Gemma in Medesano on

December 16, 1913. Carlo then brought his wife Gemma and most of his Uccellini family to America. They arrived January 1, 1914, leaving Giovanni Uccellini behind, due to an illness.

Carlo brought almost everyone he cared for with him to America. In stark contrast, Gemma was the only member of her Ferrari family who left Italy for America. Gemma left behind everything she knew and everyone she loved in Italy as she started her new life in America.

In 1914, Carlo and Gemma settled in Brooklyn, NY on Park Avenue near the Brooklyn Bridge and had their first child, Luigi (changed to Louis), born on October 11, 1914. Carlo and Gemma then moved from Brooklyn to Long Island sometime during World War I, working a farm in Woodbury, Long Island, where Nafra was born in June 1916.

In approximately 1917, the new Uccellini family moved to Central Park (that would be renamed Bethpage in 1936). They first lived in a rooming house (Nafra, called it the Parizzi House) on Broadway, the main street in Central Park. During this time Carlo and Gemma's last three children were born: a son, Werfel (changed to Frederick) in 1917 and female twins, Gemella (changed to Olga) and Genellena (changed to Elizabeth) in 1919. Thus, between October 1914 and July 1919, they would have 5 children. According to Nafra, Carlo would often brag that he had "5 kids in 4 years!"

On July 26 and 27, 1920, Carlo and Gemma purchased two adjoining land parcels between Nibbe and Schneider Lanes, just to the east of Broadway to create a small farm for the growing Uccellini family. By September 1924, Carlo built their house at the intersection of Schneider and Nibbe Lanes. They used wood from a dismantled WWI Army barracks in Camp Upton near the east end of Long Island. Except for a brief time between 1935 and 1938 when Carlo and Gemma bought a larger farm near Gardiner, in Ulster County, in Upstate New York, they lived their entire married life in the house that Carlo built in Bethpage.

Carlo was well known in and around Bethpage for his farming skills, mechanical inventions, and for working on many jobs and projects including the maintenance of the Old Motor Parkway that ran along the southern and eastern section of Bethpage (built by Vanderbilt in the early part of the 20th century).

Around 1937, Carlo was diagnosed with Parkinson's disease. After many attempts to use new treatments that falsely promised cures and only increased his agony, Carlo died on January 7, 1950. As he lay dying in a hospital, he repudiated the Catholic Church while being given his last rites by a priest called in by the family. This act added to Gemma's grief after Carlo died, and distressed her for the rest of her life.

Carlo and Gemma had bought plots at the St. Mary's Cemetery on Long Island. However, Carlo's renouncement of the Church during his last rites meant he wasn't allowed to be interred in St. Charles. Another burial site with two plots was quickly located and Carlo was buried at Amityville Cemetery on Harrison Avenue in Amityville, Long Island, New York.

Gemma led a healthy life through the 1950s and 1960s. She focused on caring for her yard, her family and her growing number of grandchildren. She became especially fond of, and bonded closely with, her grandchildren Sheila (born in 1947 to Olga) and Louis (born in 1949 to Louis and Margaret).

Sheila's tragic death in 1966 due to cancer greatly shocked and traumatized the entire family. Sheila's death was especially hard on Gemma who openly talked of her grief and asked why she wasn't taken by God instead of Sheila.

Gemma suffered a debilitating stroke in September 1970, which paralyzed her right side and left her aphasic: she could only communicate in her native Italian dialect. Gemma's eldest daughter Nafra, and her husband James Mulqueen, took on the care of Gemma in their home on Central Avenue in Bethpage for nearly 10 years, with Gemma dying peacefully in her sleep in January 11, 1980. Gemma was laid to rest next to Carlo at the Amityville Cemetery.

Carlo Uccellini

Gemma (Ferrari) Uccellini

CARLO AND GEMMA IN ITALY

Frank and Carlo Uccellini.

1: Carlo growing up in Italy

Carlo was born on July 6, 1883. Carlo's mother was Maria Rastelli and biological father was Luigi Copello. Maria Rastelli was a house cleaner in the "Villa Copelli" which was owned by the Copello family. The villa was (and still is) a large complex and includes a large two-story house that surrounds a courtyard. The complex included numerous barns, other buildings, and extensive tracts of land that surrounded the villa. The inner courtyard and surrounding main building date back to 1450, and still has a working open stove/oven built into one of the courtyard walls as observed in 1981 and 1996. Clearly, the Copello family was wealthy and secure, as the security of an Italian family in the 1800s was measured by the ownership of land. Luigi Copello was the son of the owner of the villa Copelli. He had an affair with Maria that resulted in Maria becoming pregnant with Carlo. Given the class difference between Maria Rastelli and Luigi Copello, there was no possibility of them getting married. From what my father (Louis D. Uccellini) learned during his last trip to Italy in 1986 from a private conversation with Luigi Copello's nephew (a Catholic priest in Nocelo, Italy, also named Luigi Copello), Giovanni Uccellini worked at the Villa Copelli as a gardener. Giovanni married Maria Rastelli knowing she was pregnant with Luigi Copello's baby and agreed to raise the baby as his own.

The following is based on what I learned during my first visit to Italy in 1981 and from what my father learned from his trip to Italy in 1986. The new Uccellini family, Giovanni, Maria and the baby boy named Carlo moved from the Villa Copelli to the Ferrari complex in nearby Medasari, still within the area surrounding Medesano. Carlo knew who his biological father was and he spent many hours playing and then working in and around the Villa Copelli. During my visit to the Villa Copelli in August 1981, an old neighbor from across the street was intrigued by the large number of cars that pulled up to the Villa Copelli one summer morning in a cloud of dust. After we all emerged from our cars, she walked through the cloud of dust and asked Abele Ferrari about what was going on. Abele told her that Carlo Uccellini's grandson was here to see the place where his grandfather was born. She talked to me enthusiastically and said she remembered Carlo as if it were yesterday. She said she'd played with him and thought of him as smart and very active with the children in the area.

Giovanni and Maria's family continued to grow with sons Ferdinando, Erasmo, Quinzio and daughter, Amena (Minny) born to Maria and Giovanni. Furthermore, Giovanni and Maria took in two orphaned boys: Frank and Pete. Frank (our beloved Uncle Frank Uccellini) decided to take the Uccellini name as his own and Pete Costello kept his last name.

Carlo received support from the Copello family, especially for his education, and was apparently made a promise to inherit land and related wealth from the Copello family as he entered adulthood. He was considered very intelligent by his parents and others and was educated at the top religious schools with the hope that he would become a priest. He also became very adept with his hands as a farmer, an inventor, a builder and an engineer. Carlo received a good education and could write, read and was proficient in mathematical applications at a very high level.

Carlo served his active one-year service in the Italian Army in the early 1900s. He then actively engaged in various endeavors and shops to make his living, becoming known as a builder and engineer. He seemed to be particularly interested with the bicycle as a means for enhancing his riches as he entered the 20th century, either owning or running a bicycle shop with his brothers.around or after the turn of the century

Bicycle shop – Medesano, Italy, 1902.

Frank, Frandoe, Pete (sitting) and Carlo.

The Villa Copelli: Carlo's Birthplace

Villa Copelli, inner courtyard, 1981.

Villa Copelli, 1981.

Villa Copelli, 1996. Louis W. Uccellini in foreground.

Inner Courtyard, Villa Copelli, 1996.

Business card of current owner, Villa Copelli, 1996.

Front entrance to courtyard, Villa Copelli, 1996, with current owner.

Farm area off courtyard, Villa Copelli, 1996. Susie, Abele, Fabrizio, Francesca, Giancarla, and Dominic Uccellini.

The Ferrari Crest

English Translation: One has had a sure recollection of this Modenese family ever since the 13th Century, with a man named Venturo who lived in Villa Mugnano (close to Modena) in 1271. Massimiliano I, king of the Romans, awarded this family the Title of Count Palatine by means of a diploma dated June 1st 1500. Later on, that is in 1614, Giovan Battista and Francesco obtained from the Duke of Modena the feud of Montalto (close to Reggio Emilia) and the Title of Counts.

2: Gemma growing up in Italy

From my 1981 trip to Italy and conversation with Gemma's sister Anita and Abele Ferrari (son of Gino, one of Gemma's brothers) and also meeting Ione Ferrari in Medasari (a cousin of Abele and owner of the Ferrari complex there), I was able to piece together the following story: The Ferrari's were a noble family, whose ancestors could be traced back to the thirteenth century (see the Family Shield and related translated description). By the 19ᵗʰ century, they lived in Montedigesso (near Modena) where they owned a town and surrounding lands. As Napoleon conquered Italy, he set out to persecute the rich landowners and break up their estates. Our branch of the Ferrari family moved to Celle and then after losing that land, they moved into a smaller complex in Medasari, just outside of Medesano, that had small tracts of land.

Gemma's parents were Francesco Eduardo Ferrari who married Adele Bacchini in the early 1880's. They lived in the family complex in Medasari and farmed one of those tracts of land. Francesco and Adele had four children: Gemma, Gino, Anita and Savino. Gemma was born on January 17, 1886 in the Ferrari complex (now owned by Ione Ferrari).

My visit in 1981 coincided with the renovation of the small house (like a townhouse within the longer building complex owned by the Ferrari's), including the room in which Gemma was born in. Ione presented me with the key to the old front door of the house Gemma was born in, the door that had just been replaced. Based on my notes, they all lived in the Ferrari complex until 1905, then moved to Borgo San Donnino, then to Fidenza, and onto Siccomonte. According to a news article written at the time of Gemma's brother Gino's death in 1987: "by 1911, the Ferrari family *came to the old Cantalupo hovel, previously occupied by seasonal shepherds."*

Key to the front door of house where Gemma was born.

Medasano as seen from the Ferrari complex.

Medardo and Ione Ferrari who own the Ferrari complex.

Daniela, Stafano, Giancarla, Abele and Ione Ferrari in doorway of house where Gemma was born, now being renovated.

Abele and Ione; Ferrari complex where the Uccellini's moved with Carlo.

1981 pictures of Ferrari complex where Gemma was born.

The Ferrari family was aspirational and had greater ambition for the land. With great initiative and resourcefulness, they transformed that "hovel", into an inspiring, idyllic home surrounded by a productive farm. They expanded the main farm structures on a ridgeline overlooking two stunning valleys that sloped away from the ridge in a most beautiful picturesque way. "Cantalupo" became the farm and anchor point for the Ferrari family throughout the rest of the 20th century.

By all accounts, Gemma thoroughly enjoyed her life growing up in the Ferrari complex in Medasari and she remained loyal to her family and revered her parents, an especially important trait for the eldest child in any Italian family. She did her share of the work around the farm and hunted with her brothers (and likely others). In 1981, Gemma's brothers Savino and Gino gave me her hunting bottle they had saved for the nearly 70 years since Gemma had set off for America. The bottle was carefully crafted with a tight handle that allowed it to be easily carried on hunts. The bottle also had a cooling cloth at the bottom. By placing the bottle in a creek, the cloth would become wet. This in turn would help keep the wine in the bottle cool, as the water in the cloth evaporated while the bottle was carried along on the hunt.

But by 1911, Gemma was not a happy soul during the move to Cantalupo. As we shall see, Carlo's 1906 journey to America and the sudden end to his letters completely floored her. Nevertheless, she worked with her sister and brothers to help her parents Francesco and Adele establish the Cantalupo farm. The work included tilling large fields for various grains, building barns to raise small animals, establishing beehives for the production of honey and vineyards that produced grapes of renowned quality, and planting many fruit trees that also made their orchards famous. Furthermore, Cantalupo became a well-known hunting ground, especially under the watchful eye of Gino. Gemma, Anita, Gino and Sevino each had a hollowed out region in the stone wall of the family quarters in the upstairs portion of the farm house that served as their beds. When I visited in 1981, the hunting bottle lay on Gemma's bed where the family put it after Gemma left for America in 1913. Gino and Sevino picked up the bottle and handed it to me to bring back to America, a gift I hand carried back home.

Gemma's hunting bottle.

The dance hall in Medesano where Gemma and Carlo danced that fateful night in 1903.

3: Gemma and Carlo grow up together and fall in love

As noted earlier, with the birth of Carlo, the Uccellini family moved from the Villa Copelli to the Ferrari complex in Medasari, moving into the same larger building that Gemma was born in, living two doors down from the apartment (looked like a small townhouse) that Gemma's family lived in. Thus, Carlo and Gemma knew each other as young children. Without any doubt, they played together as kids do during most of their childhood years, play that included trips to the Villa Copelli, playing and hunting in the surrounding fields, and as they grew older, working in the fields, even as Carlo attended the better schools in the area.

By the time Gemma became a teenager, she became very interested in dancing and often went to the dance hall in Medesano. According to Anita, Gemma, a tall and slender woman, was a very good and elegant dancer. Carlo went with Gemma to the dance hall one of those Saturday nights sometime in 1903. Gemma came home from that night and "was thunderstruck" according to Anita, who told me this story as if the event occurred the day before. Anita said that Gemma had the look of love in her eyes and was never the same around the Ferrari complex after that night. Clearly, the childhood relationship, the close friendship that comes from growing up and living in the same complex evolved into much more. Carlo proposed to Gemma sometime in 1904 or early 1905. By all accounts, the Ferrari family welcomed Carlo as the future husband to their oldest daughter, and this should have solidified Carlo's standing within a family that was in fact well off by Italian standards.

Nevertheless, Carlo had another dream. He dreamed of America. He read about the opportunities there. As time went on, he planned to go to America to make his mark as his own man, not dependent on the Ferrari's or the Copello's. He had a goal to raise his family in a land of the free where everyone had the opportunity to excel and accumulate the land and related riches needed to raise that family. We can only speculate on the possible reasons behind Carlo's drive to realize this dream to immigrate to America, an effort that nearly cost him the woman he loved dearly.

4. Carlo's break with Italy and the Church

As he was growing up into a young man, Carlo was embraced by the local Catholic Church, educated in the Catholic schools (which were the best schools in the area) and was apparently given the choice of which last name he would use. He chose to use the Uccellini last name of the father that cared for him over his lifetime in Italy. Then something happened that soured Carlo's relationship to the Copello family and to the church. From what I heard while in Italy in 1981, Luigi Copello was the Vicar for the local church. In this capacity, he had access to church money. It appears that, among other things, he gambled away church money. As part of the restitution, the church confiscated the land surrounding the Villa Copelli and apparently resold it to make up for the loss. With the confiscation of the land, Carlo believed he was left landless in a country where one's social status and wealth depended heavily on how much land you possessed. Carlo also came to believe that neither he nor Giovanni had the ability to care for his extended Uccellini family that was depending upon him and his genetic linkage to the Copello family for support. I did not discern any of the specifics during my first visit in 1981: when exactly this happened, how much money was lost, how much land was confiscated and exactly what the arrangement was between the Copello's and Carlo.

I was sure this happened before Carlo first left for America in 1906. My notes from my 1981 visit indicate that the Copello/church incident happened before Carlo left for America. However, my father's notes after his visit to Italy in 1986 indicate that this happened "in 1930" which I believe is more likely 1903. In any event, Carlo became bitterly disappointed about what he viewed as a broken connection to his family roots, and apparently felt denied his fair share of the Copello estate by the actions of his biological father, Luigi Copello, and by the subsequent actions of the Catholic Church. The loss of this connection to the Copello wealth was a bitter pill for Carlo, as a man without land likely would have a lifelong disadvantage, as any attempt by landless Italians would simply be stifled by the Italian caste system. On May 25, 1904, Carlo was also formally discharged from the Army after putting in his full required military service. Therefore, by the end of 1904, Carlo had broken his links to the Catholic Church and met his formal military obligations to Italy. He set his sights elsewhere, to America, the land of opportunity, a land especially well suited for a smart, driven and hardworking man like himself.

38

Ship image, La Savoie, 1906.

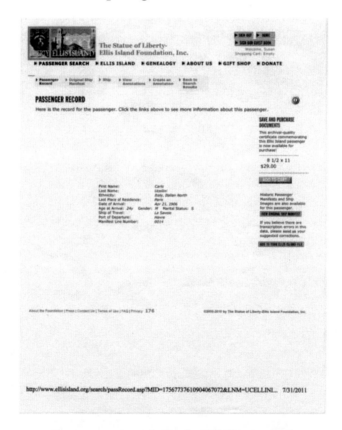

Passenger record, Carlo Ucellini, 1906.

5. Carlo leaves for America in 1906: Anita hatches her plan to break the bonds between Gemma and Carlo

By 1906, Carlo was preparing for his first voyage to America. Based on the Ellis Island Manifests, he departed from Le Havre, France on the ship *La Savoie*, arriving in New York City on April 21, 1906. As was common among the immigrants, they often traveled in groups or pairs. In this case, the manifest also show Aurelio Ucellini (age 16) traveled with Carlo's (last name also spelled Ucellini). According to my Aunt Nafra, Carlo did talk to his children about this voyage, his determination to go to America, and the need to overcome his fears. He also emphasized how crowded and cramped the quarters were on this ship and described his first view of the Statue of Liberty with awe and joy.

While Carlo settled in Brooklyn, he started working to save enough money to bring his family to American and to provide for a new and prosperous life with his intended wife, Gemma. But Gemma's sister, Anita, had other ideas.

I discovered much about Anita's plan during my first visit to Italy in 1981, which I will describe below. I stayed in the house of Gemma's brother, Gino, located down the road from Cantalupo. I met Gemma's sister, Anita, and brother, Sevino, who were all in their late 80's or early 90's. I was amazed at the clear memories they each had of their sister, Gemma, especially since they had last lived together 68 years ago! I marveled at how each one of them seemed to have this boundless energy as they did many chores, were active in loading up the wood for the upcoming winter and walked briskly about the fields.

On the second day of my stay, I was taken to Cantalupo for an afternoon and evening feast with the Ferrari family that I will never forget. Gino and Anita along with Sevino (who really was the quiet one), took me for a tour of Cantalupo: the farmhouse, the trees and area behind the house with its beehives and orchards, and the fields that spread out beyond the house and surrounding shaded area in one of the more beautiful panoramas I have ever seen, a panorama that banked up against a stand of chestnut trees off in the distance. As we walked the fields and as Giancarla translated, Anita explained how Gemma and Carlo fell in love on the dance floor in Medesano, how the family welcomed Carlo as one of their own as his intention to marry Gemma became clear. They expected that Carlo would join them in developing and working their farm. She then explained how shocked and concerned they became at Carlo's insistence that he would leave Italy, go to America and that he would take Gemma away from her family.

I finally am told of the attempt to break up Carlo and Gemma.

At this point, we stopped walking as Anita began to explain how she worked to end the relationship between Carlo and Gemma. When Carlo left for America in 1906, she described how she intercepted Carlo's letters to Gemma and stopped Gemma's letters to Carlo. Anita had insisted with Gemma that Carlo must have met someone else in America. Anita then told me how she wrote to Carlo and explained how he should stop writing to Gemma because she met someone else. The ruse worked! Gemma and Carlo both gave up, and Gemma fell into a depressed state for several years.

As Anita told me her story, both her brothers were crying, with Gino telling me of the emotional toll this whole affair took on the Ferrari family. Anita, quite determined in her plot to separate Carlo from Gemma, told this story as if it happened a year before my visit, not the 68 years before, as was the case.

Even as she told me this story, Anita became very bitter (and was still quite disappointed in herself) when she described how her effort all fell apart and Carlo and Gemma rediscovered each other in late 1912 or early 1913. As is described in the next chapter, Gemma and Carlo had again started writing letters to each other by the spring of 1913. Carlo returned to Italy in the early autumn 1913, and Carlo and Gemma then married.

All three of Gemma's siblings cried as they recounted the loss of Gemma as she left for America with her husband Carlo shortly after the wedding. Anita continued the story by noting their parents Francesco and Adele were devastated by Gemma's departure in 1914. Anita concluded that their parents died in the mid-1920's "of a broken heart."

Anita Ferrari (Gemma's sister), probably in the early 1900's.

Gemma's brothers and sister, Savino, Anita, Gino.

Fabrizio, Riccardo (son of Anita), Gino, Anita, Abele (son of Gino), Emma, Stefano in front of 43 Cabriolo, Gino's house where Abele's family lives and where Gemma and I stayed on our visits.

Gino, Anita, Savino in front of the old portion of Cantalupo, where Gemma lived before coming to America.

Gemma's brothers Gino and Savino and sister Anita in 1981.

Ricardo, Louis,
Emma, Gino, Anita
Abele, Stefano.

Gino (age 92) and
Anita (age 90)
unloading wood for the
winter.

Gemma's brother Gino and sister Anita in 1981.

43

Gemma's father, Francesco Ferrari.

Gemma's mother, Adele (Bacchini) Ferrari.

Gravestone for Gemma's mother in Siccomoni, Italy.

6: Carlo and Gemma reconnect in 1912 – 1913

So how did Carlo and Gemma reconnect after Anita's effort to separate them? As Anita told me her story of her failed attempt to separate Carlo and Gemma forever, she stated that sometime in late 1912 or early 1913, Carlo sent several posters back to the Medesano area where the Uccellini clan still resided. The poster stated that he was an Italian from the Parma area, and that he was successful in developing a stake in America that could support him and a family, and that he wanted an Italian wife from that area in Italy to share his good fortune. I often wondered how Carlo was able to send these posters back to Italy. It turns out that Giovanni Ucellini (again one "c") is listed in the Ellis Island Manifests as arriving in New York City on February 23, 1912. Recall, that 1912 is the time that Carlo sent his posters back to Italy seeking an Italian wife. I believe Giovanni's visit to New York City to see his son and his return to Italy provided the means for Carlo to send his posters back to the Parma area and his ultimate reuniting with Gemma. One of these posters was put on the bulletin board outside the dance hall in Medesano where Gemma had become thunderstruck that night long ago. Although Gemma was now living on the Cantalupo farm near Siccomonte, she apparently still made an occasional effort to go to the dance hall. Anita's story was clear. On one of the nights Gemma went to the dance hall, she saw the poster, ripped it down, brought the poster home, and immediately set about to write to Carlo. Anita stated that Gemma wrote to Carlo and basically asked: "How can this be? How can you still be available?" It wasn't long before they both realized that Anita had duped them and Anita admitted to Gemma what she had done.

We do not have copies of the letters Gemma sent to Carlo, but we do have four letters that Carlo sent to Gemma in May through September 1913, which she saved and gave to her daughter, Nafra, for safekeeping. Those letters, and the English translation provided by my friend and colleague, Franco Einaudi, are provided below. From Carlo's letters, one can feel the passion and love that still burned between them. As Franco Einaudi noted as he translated these letters for me, "your grandfather was a passionate man." Carlo was grateful for Gemma's continued interest in him and that she remained true to him despite the 6-year separation. The intense love that they had for each other becomes quite evident through the sequence of letters and Carlo's desire to marry Gemma becomes the dominant theme. Carlo at first tries to talk Gemma into coming to America to marry him. He cited his concern for the expense of him going back and forth, but more importantly he wrote of his deep concern for being called back into the Army if he returned home, as Italy stoked up their intent to attack northern Africa (specifically Libya). However, Gemma must have stuck to her guns and insisted that in order for her to marry him, Carlo would have to return to Italy and marry her there, and then as man and wife, accompany her to America. The later letters clearly show Carlo's love for Gemma and ultimately his intent to return to Italy to marry her and to return to America with her as his wife.

Brooklyn 28 May 1913

My Dear Gemma:

Why are you waiting for my arrival in Italy?

I too had thought many times about writing to you, but I did not do it because I had no intention of returning to Italy and I did not want to awake again the flame of love in you, the love that existed in the past and because I thought I would never see you again. The destiny does not allow me to leave my business here to come to see you as my sad heart would like me to do.

Please do not think about me, my dear angel, I beg you. I do not deserve you. Also, you will not be able to leave your parents.

Forgive me, Gemma, if I address you with familiarity. After receiving your letter, I have had no peace of mind. I keep thinking of the happy days we spent together and I would like to have at least your picture to be able to have a better memory of you.

I am sending a thousand affections…

Carlo

64 North Portland Ave., Brooklyn

Brooklyn 2 July 1913

Gemma my dearest,

What did you mean with the thought contained in your last letter?

Is that perhaps a message from your heart?

Are you still free? Do you still think about me, i.e., about that man who was so ungrateful towards you?

Yet, I am the one who lives in our happy memories and thinks about a happy future. Speak freely, let me have hope and do not worry about disappointing me: I deserve it (to be disappointed).

However, if a repented heart deserves a second chance, and if you are able to forgive, let me know if you would like to come here in America to embrace the man who desires you.

For the moment, I will not send you my picture because I do not have one. I will have one made as soon as possible and I will send it to you as you requested.

In fact Gemma you have always addressed me with familiarity and you must continue to do so now.

Remember me and answer since your letters are a balsam for me.

I still keep impressed in my heart your first kiss and I send you a kiss that I hope will remain impressed in your heart.

My best wishes. I would like to be able to embrace you and meld my kisses with yours. Bless you.

Yours, Carlo
64 North Portland Ave, Brooklyn, N.Y.

48

Brooklyn 6 Sept 1913

My Dear Gemma,

Last August 23 I wrote to you another letter. I am now writing again to hear from you more often.

Gemma, you cannot imagine how strong is my desire to have you. Never before I appreciated your love so much as I do now. You are the only one who has remained faithful to me and you deserve your reward (note: slightly unclear).

How happy would I be if I could have you tomorrow; but perhaps this is not possible since you may not want to leave the land where you were born in order to embrace me who lives in a foreign land. And I cannot leave this land of freedom to serve a government that I do not like.

My beloved Gemma. If it is true that you love me and that my heart can make you happy, I give you my heart. Please be strong enough to overcome the distance which separates us. I will be there at the harbor when you arrive. I will embrace you and I will make you mine at the moment you arrive, if you allow me to.

In two weeks I will go to the city to live there and I will send you my picture. If you then will decide to come here, you can come here right away. Tell your father to pay for your trip and that I will pay him back. If he cannot do it, write back right away. I will take care of everything myself.

Get the birth certificate for me and for yourself. You will see that we will enjoy the happiness that we have been waiting for so long. I kiss you. Yours for life.

Carlo

Greetings to your parents and give a kiss to my mother when you see her.

Brooklyn 29 September 1913

My love:

Your eloquent letter gives me a great deal of confidence. I believe I have found in you the woman I have been looking for for a long time. But how can we succeed in getting together (note: the actual word here is possessive you). However, if you will understand me, if what you write will really say what is in your heart, if you will really want to get together with me and for our family, if you will carefully reflect upon what I am writing, then you will be able to take a decision. (note: the following sentence is too long and have to ready it up in several sentences.)

I love you with all my strength, as I have never loved anyone else in my life. I never understood the need to love as I do now; however, at the same time, I have to say that one cannot live of love alone. You must think of this point, too. I am not being naughty if I say I cannot come to Italy. If I came, I would run the risk of having to spend 2 years time in the military service and would have to pay 1500 lire for a round trip for me and a one way trip for you. This is so because I cannot remain in Italy. I do not like to live there. Please keep in mind this point in my interest as well as yours.

If you decide to be mine, I do not ask of you anything else but that you will love me and be faithful. I do not worry about the good and bad things of the past. I understand very well what you are writing and we could continue to communicate via letters.

Page 2

I am looking for a companion. Destiny wanted that I met you and that I fell in love with you. If you like me too, then you know what you need to do: write to me and I will send you the money (or the ticket) for the trip and I will be waiting for you.

If on the other hand you have doubts and you are afraid that I may offend you (note: somewhat unclear here) then I can lend you the money to come to the United States where you will be free to do what you want. Women here find jobs very easily, in fact they are in great demand. Once here if you do not like to become my wife, you will be able to earn quickly enough money to return to Italy. If, on the other hand, what you write is exactly what you feel, then you can become mine even before you leave the ship. You would not lose your honor since I do not see anything wrong in falling into the arms of someone whom you love and who loves you.

Please make a decision. It is too long that we are apart. Let our hearts free to express themselves. Let us take advantage of the pleasure that God gives those who love each other and who are faithful to each other. Do not prevent things from happening. I am waiting for you.

Have a sincere kiss from your Carlo.

Gemma (date unknown probably around 1906 - 1910.)

These may be the pictures that Carlo and Gemma exchanged in the course of their correspondence.

Province of Parma
Township of Borgo San Donnino
Town of Medesano

Extract from Wedding Register for the year 1913, No.35, Part 1.

Uccellini, Carlo and Ferrari, Gemma; the year 1913, December 16, at 2 o'clock in the city hall of Medesano, open to the public, in front of me, Zaccarini, Raimondo, common assessor, acting for the absent Mayor, Officier of Civil State, dressed in official uniform, have personally appeared, first: Uccellini, Carlo single, age 30 years, blacksmith, born in Borgo San Donnino, resident in Medesano, son of Giovanni, resident in Medesano and Rastelli Maria, resident in Medesano; Second: Ferrari, Gemma single, age 28 years, housegirl, born in Medesano, resident in Borgo San Donnino. Both requested me to marry them. To this effect they presented me all the documents described underneath: from the examination of them and the one produced before for the request of publication, said document examined by me, inserted in the volume of the supplement of this register, resulting in no obstacle in the celebration of matrimony. I read to them the article 130, 131, and 132 of the Civil Code. Then I asked the groom if he intends to take for his wife the here present Ferrari, Gemma. I ask Ferrari, Gemma if she takes for her husband the here present Uccellini, Carlo. As both answered in affirmative in full consciousness of what they were saying, also the witnesses underwritten, I pronounce in the name of the law that both shall be united in matrimony. At this act has been present Zilioli, Massimo age 32 years, mechanic and Barbieri, Carlo age 33 years, vegetable grower, both residents in this town. The documents presented are the certificates of publication made in Medesano two successive Sundays, the 23rd of November and the 30th of November of the current year. The 30th of November and the 7th of December respectively. Read the present act, then they all signed except Barbieri, who doesn't know how to write. Undersign: Uccellini, Carlo; Ferrari, Gemma; Zilioli Massimo; and R. Zaccarini. Uniform Copy. Medesano, December 17, 1913.

Officier of the Civil State,
Gepe Dodettena

Translated by Carlo Uccellini, August 19, 1943

Carlo Uccellini

Subscribed and sworn to before me at
Bethpage, New York.

Aug. 20th. 1943

Harry A. Leoz

Notary Public

Nassau Q. ny

Extract of Wedding Register, Uccellini wedding on December 16, 1913; translated by Carlo Uccellini on August 19, 1943.

7: Carlo returns to Italy, marries Gemma and brings his family to America

Carlo returned to Italy in the early autumn in 1913 and married Gemma in the City Hall in Medesano on December 16, 1913. The marriage was officiated by Raimondo Zaccarini (a common assessor standing in for the absent Mayor) and witnessed only by acquaintances Massimo Ziliola and Carlo Barbieri. From Carlo's own description of the wedding provided in 1943, it is clear that no one from either family attended the wedding. Within days, Carlo then collected his family and arranged for them all to come back to America with him. The Ellis Island Manifest shows that Carlo, "Germira" (Gemma), "Quinzro" (Quinzio), "Erminio" (Amena) (Carlo's sister, called Minnie in America) and (Carlo's Mother) Marie Ucellini "Restelli" (Rastelli) departed Southampton, England in late December 1913 and all arrived in New York City on January 1, 1914 on the ship "New York" (American Line - White Star Line, Ship Company). Evardo Restelli (a relative to Maria?) is also listed on this manifest. One interesting aspect of the manifest is the consistency of the spelling of Ucellini with one "c". One person who never made it back to America to stay with Carlo and Gemma's family was Giovanni Uccellini who, according to my father's notes, was too ill to travel at that time. Luigi Copello's nephew, Monsignor Luigi Copello told my father during his last visit to Italy in 1986, that Giovanni was sick and could not travel in late 1913 or early 1914. Unfortunately, the window on immigration to America slammed shut with the growing belligerence in Europe and then the onset of World War I in August 1914. From this perspective, it is clear that Carlo and Gemma just made it out of Italy at the right time, and that if they had waited even a few months, Carlo's fears about being pulled back into Italy's war plans would have panned out. Carlo, Gemma and the rest would not have made it to America.

With their arrival in New York City on January 1, 1914, Carlo moved his entire family to America (except for Giovanni). On the other hand, Gemma left her entire loving family behind in Italy. Giovanni would die alone in Italy on July 21, 1921 and be buried in Medesano (with the last name spelled Ucellini again with one "c").

56

The Statue of Liberty-
Ellis Island Foundation, Inc.

► **PASSENGER SEARCH** ► **ELLIS ISLAND** ► **GENEALOGY** ► **ABOUT US** ► **GIFT SHOP** ► **DONATE**

▸ Passenger Record	▸ Original Ship Manifest	▸ Ship	▸ View Annotations	▸ Create an Annotation	▸ Back to Search Results

SHIP IMAGE

You can purchase this image and information by clicking "Add to Shopping Cart."

* Please note that ship images are smaller than the acid-free archival paper they are printed on. The ship image on 11" X 17" paper measures approximately 9" X 12". The ship image on 8 1/2" X 11" paper measures approximately 5" X 7". Measurements are approximate only. Our customized frames are guaranteed to fit every document.

The New York

Associated Passenger	Date of Arrival	Port of Departure
Ucellini, Carlo	Jan 01, 1914	Southampton

Purchase this item
Choose a size:

8 1/2x11   (Small 5x7 Ship Image)
$10.00

11x17   (Large 9x12 Ship Image)
Fits Document Holder
$12.50

[ADD TO CART]

Built by J. & G. Thomson Limited, Glasgow, Scotland, 1888. 10,499 gross tons; 560 (bp) feet long; 60 feet wide. Steam triple expansion engines, twin screw. Service speed 20 knots. 1,740 passengers (540 first class, 200 second class, 1,000 third class).Clipper stem, three funnels and three masts.

Built for Inman & International Steamship Company, in 1888 and named **City of New York**. Liverpool-New York service. World's fastest ship 1892-93. Sold to American Line, in 1893 and renamed **New York**. Southampton to New York service. Renamed **USS Harvard** in 1898. Served briefly for US Navy in 1898 during the Spanish-American war. Returned to American Line, in 1898 and reverted to **New York**. Southampton to New York service. Renamed **USS Plattsburg** in 1918. Armed merchant cruiser service. Sold in 1920 and reverted to **New York**. to Polish Navigation Company. New York-Danzig service. New York-Mediterranean service in 1922. Scrapped at Genoa in 1923.

Photo: Peabody Essex Museum

**Ship manifest for Carlo and Gemma's voyage to America, December 1913.
Arrived January 1, 1914.**

The Statue of Liberty-
Ellis Island Foundation, Inc.

► SIGN OUT   ► HOME
► SIGN OUR GUEST BOOK
Welcome, Susan
Shopping Cart: Empty

► PASSENGER SEARCH   ► ELLIS ISLAND   ► GENEALOGY   ► ABOUT US   ► GIFT SHOP   ► DONATE

► Passenger   ► Original Ship   ► Ship   ► View   ► Create an   ► Back to
  Record   Manifest   Annotations   Annotation   Search
                                                                              Results

PASSENGER RECORD

Here is the record for the passenger. Click the links above to see more information about this passenger.

First Name:	*Carlo*
Last Name:	*Ucellini*
Ethnicity:	*Italy, Italian North*
Last Place of Residence:	*New York, U. S. A.*
Date of Arrival:	*Jan 01, 1914*
Age at Arrival: *30y* Gender: *M* Marital Status: *M*	
Ship of Travel:	*New York*
Port of Departure:	*Southampton*
Manifest Line Number:	*0001*

SAVE AND PURCHASE DOCUMENTS

This archival-quality certificate commemorating this Ellis Island passenger is now available for purchase!

....

8 1/2 x 11
$29.00

....

ADD TO CART

Historic Passenger Manifests and Ship Images are also available for this passenger.

VIEW ORIGINAL SHIP MANIFEST

If you believe there are transcription errors in this data, please send us your suggested corrections.

ADD TO YOUR ELLIS ISLAND FILE

http://www.ellisisland.org/search/passRecord.asp?MID=17567737610904067072&LNM=UCELLINI... 7/31/2011

Passenger record for Carlo and Gemma's voyage to America, December 1913.
Arrived January 1, 1914.

Maria (Rastelli) Uccellini, Carlo's mother.

Giovanni Ucellini gravestone; Medesano, Italy.

Italian friends make the USA voyage

An interesting listing in the Ellis Island Manifest is that a Eugenio Bellin (Eugene Bellini) and Erasini (Erasmo) Uccellini arrived in New York from the same Parma area in northern Italy on July 23, 1913. The Bellini's were very close friends with the Uccellini's in Italy. As recounted in notes provided by Gene (Eugene) Bellini to me in the late 1990's, his father (Alberto) knew Carlo as childhood friends and that they told a story of how Carlo saved Alberto's life by rescuing Alberto from drowning in a lake near their home in Italy. Nafra also recounted this story for me, that Carlo jumped into the lake and saved Alberto from drowning.

From information provided by Albert Bellini, Alberto Bellini arrived in America with his wife Irma on May 18, 1904 (on the ship *Citta di Napoli*). The Bellini's immigration to America in 1904 was likely a draw for Carlo to make his first cross-Atlantic transit in 1906. The Bellini's remained close friends to the Uccellini clan through this and future generations. As we grew up in Bethpage in the 1950's and 1960's, we (the Uccellini's and Mulqueen's) always thought of the older Bellini "kids" (Barbara, Albert and Audrey) as our cousins and Gene and Winnie Bellini as an uncle and aunt.

Furthermore, according to an interview with Perry DeLalio (Appendix IV), a significant number of Italians from the Medesano area settled in and around Bethpage and Farmingdale area. They remained lifelong friends with Carlo, Gemma and the Uccellini family. *"Medesano was the heart and soul of the this group."* Perry DeLalio also emphasized that these families looked up to Carlo as *"the go-to man"* who could build or fix anything and that *"Carlo was a very smart man"* who would translate Itallian to English and vice-versa; an important ability when ensuring all legal papers were in order for Italian community.

8: Cantalupo, paradise and the Ferrari family Gemma left behind

Below are pictures of Cantalupo taken during my visits in 1981 and 1996 that capture the richness and beauty of the land and family that Gemma left behind. The importance of Cantalupo to the area and the Ferrari family is captured at the end of this chapter in the article on Gino Ferrari published after he died.

Cantalupo
The Saturday
Feast

Mariam in the blue blouse standing behind Adele

Cantalupo, the Saturday feast, 1981.

Gino
Anita
Sevino

Barn at

Cantalupo

Sevino, Adele
(daughter of Gino)
Fabrizio, Anita

at the Bocchi court.
Vero, Emiliano, Stefano.

Cantalupo, 1981.

Fields of Cantalupo, 1996.

Bee hives at Cantalupo, 1996.

Dino, Susan Uccellini, Francesca, Giancarla. 1996.

Barns at Cantalupo, 1996.

Dominic, Francesca, Anthony Uccellini at Cantalupo, 1996;
Emilio (back) and Dino are Carlo and Gemma's nephews.

Setting up for afternoon feast at Cantalupo, 1996.   Louis Uccellini in vineyard at Cantalupo.

Gemma's bed alcove area at Cantalupo (1996).

Savino, Anita, and Gino (1985).

July 18th 1986

Dear Lois, Susie & Kids,

We hope you all are fine. We should have written to you before, and are sorry about that, but I was sent to Bologna to examine students who took the General Certificate of Education and I stayed there a month.

The bad news we have to communicate is that Gino died on June 16th, even though he had managed to recover after the first signs of his desease. In fact, after we last wrote to you, he was again on his feet, and he was able to enjoy his 97th birthday. There was a big celebration, and all of his grandchildren were around him. He was even able to blow out all the candles on his big birthday cake. Fabrizio recorded a video-cassette on that day, and we sent a copy of it to your father & mother, so you'll be able to see it when you visit them!

Giancarla's letter informing us of Gino's death in July 1986.

Unfortunately, he grew worse, and soon he was forced to stay in bed again. He completely lost his appetite and he became extremely lean and weak, and also had breathing problems. Eventually, the combination of all of these deseases led him to death. When he died, all of his sons & daughter were with him, and he died as a patriarch, as he had always lived, in a sort of unchanging world. Anita and Savino weren't told about their brother's death at once, but only after the funeral. The news was quite a shock for them, because they had always stuck together to face the passing of years, and found strenght to survive in one another. The funeral was officiated on the 18th of June; there were a lot of people, and cars all along the road down the hill. Now Gino lies in Fidenza cemetery, next to his wife. On the local newspaper an article was published about "The Contalupo Patriarch", and we sent it to your parents.

We know you will feel sorry about his death, because you appreciated and respected the values Gino and his brother and sisters stood for. We know that meeting these old people has been a meaningful experience both for you and your father. Abele is now looking for a flat in Fidenza (I think Gino's house will be sold), to be closer to his sons.

We miss you, and we can't help thinking about last year when we were in America. I should say that we remember every detail of our visit even more neatly now, after one year, people and places. Thank you for Dominic's picture: he is handsome! Our love to the kids. We wish you a wonderful summer, and let's keep in touch waiting for next time we'll see one another.

Love,
Giancarla

We enclose Gino's photo made for the funeral.
Love
Daniel e Stefano.

GINO FERRARI, SPENTOSI ALL'ETÀ DI 97 ANNI

Il patriarca di Cantalupo

Instancabile, era abile in tutto: caccia, viticoltura, agricoltura, frutticoltura, lavori artigianali – Buono ma severo, durante la degenza all'ospedale trovò la forza di redarguire il figlio (66 anni!) per un ritardo nei lavori in vigna

Quanti fidentini, anche di una certa età, saprebbero dire con sicurezza dove si trova quel sito in zona collinare chiamato Cantalupo? Senz'altro pochini, mentre la maggior parte ne ignorerà perfino il nome; in effetti, percorrendo solo strade ordinarie, nessuno lo troverebbe.

Occorre portarsi a Siccomonte Alto e invece di proseguire per Tabiano, svoltare attorno a una maestà campestre e, dopo un bel chilometro di carrareccia scomoda e sassosa su terreno ondulato, si giunge a uno strano casale immerso in un boschetto di olmi e querce.

È Cantalupo, dal nome del rio che scorre nel Fondovalle, e questo è stato, per mezzo secolo, il regno di Gino Ferrari, scomparso la settimana scorsa, alla rispettabile età di anni 97. Esempio piuttosto raro di una lunga vita, vissuta intensamente fino all'ultimo respiro.

Staccatasi da Medesano nel 1906, e dopo una permanenza di qualche anno in quel di Borgo S. Donnino, la sua famiglia approdò alla vecchia bicocca di Cantalupo, occupata in precedenza da pastori stagionali. Gino, soldato di leva nel 1909, col richiamo del 1911 si trovò in Libia a combattere contro l'impero turco; a Tobruck, in un'azione contro truppe libiche, una palla di fucile lo colpì all'anca sinistra e lo rispedì in patria. Questa palla di piombo, mai estratta, se l'è tenuta per tutta la vita, e allo scoppio della guerra 1915-18 gli ha consentito di evitare il fronte, di essere richiamato in servizio territoriale e di prendere moglie.

Sempre nel vecchio Cantalupo, morti i genitori, Gino e il fratello Savino (tuttora vivente) allevarono le loro famigliole, aggiungendo nuove costruzioni man mano che la crescita dei figli richiedeva spazio. La carriera di cacciatore Gino l'aveva iniziata, ancora sedicenne, col padre (prima licenza di caccia: 1906). Negli anni seguenti partiva con Savino e con una muta di segugi per partecipare a battute alla lepre assieme ai cacciatori più rinomati di Fidenza (vedi foto). La selvaggina era tanta, i cacciato-

gli artefici di tanta grazia erano «I Ferári d'Cantalup».

Gino Ferrari ha praticato e trasmesso ai figli Abele ed Emilio anche l'esperienza dell'apicoltore. Non in senso pedestre, per raccogliere a caso ciò che si deposita dell'arnia, ma apicoltura d'élite, con la cura meticolosa degli sciami e la selezione del prodotto. Il biondo miele di acacia che estraggono dai favi in primavera è di qualità superiore.

Abilissimo innestatore di viti e piante da frutta, l'ho sorpreso nell'aprile del 1984 mentre praticava alcuni innesti su un melo del vicino Armellini; osservandolo bene, ho finalmente capito come va eseguito un innesto a corona! Instancabile, trovava sempre il modo di utilizzare il tempo; la sua fida roncola, spesso smarrita e sempre ritrovata, ne sa qualche cosa. E se il clima lo costringeva al chiuso, diventava artigiano: usando virgulti di salice costruiva ceste e robusti canestri, mentre col sorgo confezionava eleganti scope e scopini (i «smalsarén»).

Molto attaccato alla famiglia, è stato «rezdor» buono, arguto, ma ben risoluto e autoritario, le cui decisioni moglie e figli non credevano proprio di dovere discutere. Questo scettro l'ha tenuto saldamente fino in ultimo: tre mesi fa, degente all'ospedale, tra una crisi e l'altra, trovò il fiato per redarguire il figlio Dino (66 anni) perché in ritardo nella potatura e sistemazione della vigna. Se fosse sopravvissuto fino a ottobre, il via per le operazioni di vendemmia, prima per le uve bianche, poi per le rosse, l'avrebbe dato ancora lui, e con sicurezza!

R. B.

Nelle foto di Banzola (1932): Gino Ferrari è il 4° da sinistra. Si distinguono: Bernardi (Pir), Mambriani, Monteverdi, il farmacista Gino Ferrari e il figlio Angelo.

GINO FERRARI
N. 27-4-1889   M. 19-6-1986

La sua memoria cara rivivrà eternamente nell'animo di quanti lo conobbero e gli vollero bene.
I suoi cari a perenne ricordo.

IMPRESA FUNEBRE BONELLI FID.

The article is by Engineer R. Bravi; I think you met him in Cantalupo

Gino Ferrari died at the age of 97. THE CANTALUPO PATRIARCH.

Never tired, he was skilled in many fields: hunting, vine-growing, agricolture, fruit growing, handicraft. Good though strict, when he was in hospital he found the strenght to reproach his son (aged 66) since he was late with the vineyard works.

How many inhabitants of Fidenza could say where the hilly site call_ ed Cantalupo is? We are sure they are very few, and most of them will even ignore its name; actually, running trough ordinary roads, nobody could find it. One should go to Siccomonte Alto and, instead of going towards Tabiano, one should make a turn and, after a good Kilometre of an uncomfortable stony country lane on a hilly ground, one comes to a strange farmhouse surrounded by a wood of oaks and elms. That is Cantalupo, named after the creek running down in the valley. That had been, for over a century, Gino Ferrari's reign, who died last week at the respectable age of 97. Quite a rare example of a long life, intensely lived till the last breath.

Having left Medesano in 1906, and after staying in Borgo San Donnino for a few years, his family came to the old Cantalupo hovel, previously occupied by seasonal shepherds. Gino, a conscript in 1909, was recalled in 1911 and was in Libya fighting against the Turkish Empire; in Tobruk, during an action against LibYan Troups, a bullet hit him at his hip and he was sent home. This bullet was never extracted and allowed him to avoid going to the front at the outbreak of 1915-18 War, to be called up for territory service and to get married.

Still in old Cantalupo, after his parents' death Gino and his brother Savino (still living) raised their families, adding up new buildings as the children grew up and needed more room. Gino started his hunting carreer with his father, when he was 16. (His first hunting license was dated 1906). In the following years he used to go hare-shooting with Savino, their dogs and Fidenza's most famous hunters (see picture). The hunting seasons were profitable: up to 190 hares a season. In the 30's the two brothers were known as "i Fereri d'Cantalup" and Gino renewed his last hunting license in 1983.

Partial English translation of newspaper article about Gino and Cantalupo provided by R. Bravi, 1986

CARLO AND GEMMA IN AMERICA

9: Carlo and Gemma start up in America

With their arrival in New York City on January 1, 1914, Carlo and Gemma set about establishing their new "home" in Brooklyn. From his letters to Gemma, we can see that Carlo had lived on 64 Portland Avenue right near the Brooklyn Bridge. Upon their arrival in America as a married couple, Carlo and Gemma settled in a different apartment on nearby Park Avenue, also in Brooklyn. Today, both of the addresses lie directly underneath the Brooklyn-Queens Expressway (Interstate 278) that Robert Moses built right through this neighborhood (as he generally did throughout New York City in the 1930's through the 1960's). On October 11, 1914, Gemma gave birth to their first child, a son they named Luigi Domenico Uccellini (later changed to Louis Dominick), my father. He often told us that he was born "right under the Brooklyn Bridge," which is not too much of an exaggeration given that they lived within a half mile of the bridge.

The period of time in Brooklyn was not discussed much with the grandchildren growing up in the 1940's and 1950's. From history books, we know that the Italian working class that lived in the bigger American cities was not treated well before, during and after World War I. The discriminatory attitudes directed at Italians during and after the turn of the century were compounded by Italy fighting on the wrong side at the beginning of World War I. The Red Scare after the Russian Revolution in 1917-1918 and the ongoing fear of the post-WWI anarchy movement in the United States (and the increase in indiscriminate bombings in major US cities) made the discriminatory behavior against Italian immigrants (and others living in the poorer sections) even worse. I remember being told a story that Gemma did have a job after she arrived in America, working long hours in a clothing factory, a so-called "sweat shop." When she asked for or cried out "acqua," the floor boss would sternly answer back "In English." Only when she understood that she had to ask for "water," did she get it. Gene Bellini described growing up in Brooklyn as a tough experience with Gene and his friends always having to fight back those who hurled many insults at them (Gene seemed especially upset at being called a "WOP" an epithet which is short for "without papers").

Carlo and Gemma's family at home that Carlo built at the intersection of Schneider Lane and Nibbe Lane, Bethpage; photo dated 1928. From left to right: their automobile, Gemma, Elizabeth, Louis, Fred, Olga, Nafra and Carlo.

The large room they are standing in front of is facing southwest; the family called it the "sun room." Note all the windows. It was a very sunny, enjoyable room in the spring, summer and fall. The rest of the house consisted of a lower floor with left side living room and dining room. On the right side was a sewing room, bathroom, and kitchen to the rear. The kitchen side entrance can be seen on right. The upper floor had four bedrooms, one bathroom and one small room.

10: Carlo and Gemma and family settle in Central Park, Long Island

By 1915, Carlo and Gemma with one child in tow, decided to move out of Brooklyn onto Long Island, near the town of Woodbury where their first daughter, Nafra was born on June 28, 1916. Nafra recalled (in her Oral History for the Bethpage Historical Society) that she came to Central Park when she was about a year to a year and a half old. Central Park was an unincorporated small town in east-central Nassau County in the Township of Oyster Bay (the name of the town Central Park was changed to Bethpage in 1936). Woodbury and Central Park were areas that were becoming magnets for many other Italians to live and work. Carlo worked as a farmer at various truck farms near Central Park and Woodbury, but quickly settled on Central Park as the place where he would raise his family. Among many attributes related to the small town life, Central Park was the site of a train station for the developing Long Island Railroad, thus providing easy transportation to and from New York City. The last three Uccellini children were born in Central Park in central Long Island.

Nafra and Louis told the story that Carlo was known to brag that he "Had 5 kids in 4 years!" with an obvious sense of pride. Louis was born October 11, 1914 in Brooklyn; Nafra was born June 28, 1916 in Woodbury, Long Island. Gemma and Carlo's last three children were born in Central Park. Werfel (Frederick) born October 30, 1917; twins, Gemmella (Olga) and Genellena (Elizabeth) were born July 27, 1919. Olga and Elizabeth were born in the rented house on Broadway (that Nafra recalled as the Parizzi House) right near the intersection of Nibbe Lane, Schneider Lane and Broadway.

By 1919 or 1920, Carlo set his sights on two adjacent parcels of land (about three acres) just off Broadway and between Nibbe and Schneider Lanes. The deeds kept by Lenard Mulqueen (President of the Central Park Historical Society, Carlo and Gemma's grandson and current owner of their house) show that they purchased two adjacent parcels: from Elenor Dehler to Charles Uccellini on July 26,1920 and from Anne Knoblauch to Charles Uccellini on July 27, 1920.

Several years later, Carlo took advantage of an effort by the US Army to dismantle a fort in Upton, New York located on the eastern end of Long Island. The fort was built for housing and training soldiers who would fight in Europe during World War I. With the sudden and unexpected end to the war, the Army set out to dismantle the housing that was no longer needed. Carlo and his helpers (likely Uncle Frank and his other brothers) drove out to Upton (a long arduous drive in those days) and loaded up several trucks with enough lumber to build a two-story house on the farm right near the intersection of Nibbe and Schneider Lanes, with a view of Broadway less than a block away.

Carlo built a wood frame and board house and then covered the outer layer with stucco. The house was completed in 1923 according to Nafra (Oral history from Central Park Historical Society). Dianne's notes from her conversation with Nafra provide insight to their move into the new house. "My father built the house on Schneider Lane. And we moved into the house before it was completed. All the children slept in what was then the dining room with a big pot belly stove in it. Mom and dad slept in what was later the living room. After making changes in the plans, I remember mostly the changes of the stairway to the second floor, which later became the pantry."

Apparently, Nafra was indicating that the original plans for the house were changed as Carlo was building it. Nafra crossed out her original sentence "after making changes on the plans" in her notes to Dianne.

Title insurance for the house was purchased for $725 on September 9, 1924. It was here that Carlo and Gemma would settle down after their long journey and raise their family.

By the next year, Carlo would become an American citizen through naturalization procedures administered by the Supreme Court of Nassau County on October 3, 1925. It was not until January 7, 1944 that Gemma became a naturalized citizen.

Carlo's Naturalization Certificate, October 3, 1925

THE UNITED STATES OF AMERICA

ORIGINAL
TO BE GIVEN TO
THE PERSON NATURALIZED

CERTIFICATE OF NATURALIZATION

No. 5771915

Petition No 23822

Personal description of holder as of date of naturalization. Age 58 years; sex Female color White complexion Light color of eyes Gray color of hair Gray height 5 feet 2 inches weight 113 pounds, visible distinctive marks None

Marital status Married former nationality ITALIAN

I certify that the description above given is true, and that the photograph affixed hereto is a likeness of me

X Gemma uccellini
(Complete and true signature of holder)

STATE OF NEW YORK } ss:
COUNTY OF NASSAU

Be it known, that at a term of the Supreme Court of Nassau County held pursuant to law at Mineola, New York on January 7, 1944 the Court having found that GEMMA UCCELLINI then residing at Snyder's Lane, Bethpage, N. Y. intends to reside permanently in the United States (when so required by the Naturalization Laws of the United States), had in all other respects complied with the applicable provisions of such naturalization laws, and was entitled to be admitted to citizenship, thereupon ordered that such person be and (s)he was admitted as a citizen of the United States of America.

In testimony whereof the seal of the court is hereunto affixed this 7th day of January, in the year of our Lord nineteen hundred and forty-four, and of our Independence the one hundred and sixty-eighth.

Seal

CHAS. E. RANSOM

(It is a violation of the U.S. Code (and punishable as such) to copy, print, photograph, or otherwise illegally use this certificate

Clerk of the SUPREME Court

By ___ Deputy Clerk

DEPARTMENT OF JUSTICE

Gemma's Naturalization Certificate, January 7, 1944

**Central Park School
Kindergarten 1921**

I am at the extreme left. My brother, Louis Uccellini is on the top row at the extreme right.

Central Park School Kindergarten, 1921. (provided by Nafra.)

Louis Uccellini

Nafra Uccellini

When I was in high school, there was only one bus to the Farmingdale High School. We all met for the bus at Al Bogners stationary shop at Broadway and Baldwin Place. Mr. Louis Maggi drove the bus.

Powell Avenue School picture, 1922. (Provided by Nafra.)

11: Family life in Central Park/Bethpage

By all accounts, this was a very close knit Italian family where the children revered their parents. Carlo was a dominant presence who could be stern but his children remembered him as enjoying them immensely.

When Carlo and Gemma's children were young, Italian was spoken almost exclusively at home, though English was learned and used outside the house. This reliance on Italian actually worked against my father, Louis, who was so shy and his English so poor that he did not go to grammar school at the Powell Avenue School until his sister Nafra was old enough to go. He then went to school with Nafra, holding her hand along the way.

My father and Nafra graduated from grammar school, with Nafra recounting to Dianne: 'Upon my graduation from grammar school we (Carlo and Nafra) walked into town where he bought me a Waterman pen. How I wish I still had it." Neither Nafra nor Louis graduated from high school as the depression set in in the early 1930s; though Nafra may have gone to high school for a year or so. Frederick, Olga and Elizabeth did graduate from Farmingdale High School, the only high school that served Central Park (Bethpage) at the time. The name of the town was changed from Central Park to Bethpage in 1936.

With the purchase and development of their own farm in Central Park, Carlo began designing farm machinery and developing a reputation (in town) as an inventor. Perry Delalio describes in a short note in a Monthly Newsletter from the Central Park Historical Society, and recalled by Dianne, one of his most noted inventions was called the "Carrot Washer." It was actually a "root washer," a cylindrical, wood-slatted machine with spaces between the slats. The large machine was turned by hand while another person hosed water through the machine to clean the vegetables.

Carlo also filed a patent on November 7, 1922 (see Appendix II) for a pelt treating and cleaning machine (Patent number 1,434,932). Carlo also had a reputation for working expertly with sheet metal. According to a story my father told Lenard, he attempted to build a perpetual motion device, a challenge he took on for almost a decade. There were several family stories about Grandpa having a maintenance job for the Old Motor Parkway that was the first freeway on Long Island, built by Vanderbilt in the early part of the Century for weekend racing events that involved Vanderbilt and his friends. The Old Motor Parkway ran along the southern and eastern boundary of Central Park. Carlo operated a steamroller that was used to maintain a smooth surface in a roadbed that quickly developed potholes from heavy use and rainstorms. Later, Carlo made fuel for racing cars in a distillation system he set up in the barn, fuel that was used by racers at the newly constructed Freeport Raceway.

Central Park Historical Society

P. O. Box 178

Bethpage, N.Y. 11714-0178

CENTRAL PARK HISTORICAL SOCIETY NEWSLETTER

JULY/AUGUST - 2006

IT IS GREAT HEARING FROM YOU - We received the following letter from **Perry DeLalio:** " I have just received the May issue of your newsletter and, as usual, it stirred up old memories of Central Park/Bethpage. Anna Lee Tallman Emery is correct, if you start to really think, you could write a book. I remember Anna Lee coming to the farm because, if I am correct, her mother and my mother went to school together in Brooklyn. As usual, the families from the Parma area (Italy) remained friends in America.

I remember Jack Norris and Troop 159. Joe Ryan was chairman for a time then I was for awhile too. However, the success of Troop 159 was the scout master Wesly Brush, George Ray and Dave Klem. Then we had Walter Looney as Advancement or Merit Badge Chairman and Walter Barsett - Finance Chairman. At the last meeting in June when awards were handed out, we always had an inspirational speech by either Francis Looney or Harold Looney. Our troop had over 50 boys, and some we had to turn down because we could not handle more. We went to Camp Onteora in Livingston Manor, New York for two weeks and Operation Igloo in February for five days. When Tony Trapani was studying for the priesthood, he would come to Onteora for two weeks and lead the troop each evening in song strumming his guitar. He was our jewel and he was loved.

However, the real story I want to recall is the one about Carlo Uccellini and his two boys, Louis and I believe the other boy was Fred. Louis was my friend till he passed away. Anyway, Carlo invented a root washer for the farmers. It was a boon to all farmers who used it. It tripled the production of washed carrots and parsnips. I will try to describe it because we had one. Mr. Uccellini with his two boys made many of them in his garage in Bethpage. If you can picture a 1000 gallon drum cut in half as the base, then a slatted barrel was made to fit inside riding on greased bearings. At one end there was a trough where you dumped the root products into the slotted wood barrel which was laying in the steel tank filled with water. A big fly wheel turned the barrel in the water till it washed the product. It was hooked to a water cooled pump or a tractor fly wheel with a leather belt. When the root vegetables were washed, a steel gate was opened at the other end and the washed product spilled out to another trough then into bushel baskets. Mr. Uccellini had boards inside the wooden barrel angled to force the product out the front. It was truly a great piece of farm equipment. Louis and Fred went on to be prime mechanics for the war effort in the 40's. Louis was always proud of Walter's undertakings in Troy."

We thank Perry for his great memories of Central Park/Bethpage. I am sure this will jog the memories of many proud farmers who farmed the land in our area. Also, some good memories of the Boy Scouts of Bethpage.

Recollection from Perry DeLalio in Central Park Historical Society Newsletter, July/August 2006 recalling Carlo Uccellini's "Root Washer".

Uccellini
Root Washing Machine
Central Park, NY
Photo taken between 1917-1935

Grandpa was an inventor! When I was young, some of the old timers in Bethpage would speak respectfully of my Grandfather. They told the story of some of his skills and inventions. They said that he invented the root washing machine but that the "patent was stolen."

Grandfather Uccellini did obtain a patent document for a pelt cleaning machine. My mother Nafra Mulqueen still has that document.

To the family, Grandpa's invention was known as the "carrot washing machine. I remember that in about 1949, when I was about 8 years old, there was one carrot washing machine in the old barn. The oldest grandchildren enjoyed playing in the barns. We would take turns climbing into the drum of the washer, another child would turn the crank. The child inside the drum then had a ride that was "topsy-turvy". It was our very own amusement ride.

by Dianne Mulqueen Sullivan
Granddaughter of Carlo Uccellini
September 9, 1999

Dianne Mulqueen Sullivan remembering her grandfather's "root washing" machine.

EXPRESS CARROT WASHER

It is cheap when you buy,
It is cheap when you run,
It washes all your carrots
Just like having great fun;
It pays for itself in a very short run.

CARLO UCCELLINI
CENTRAL PARK, N. Y.

Sales brochure for Carlo's carrot washer. According to Perry DeLalio interview (Appendix 4), this picture is taken at the DeLalio farm with his father Pierro DeLalio in the back and Lorenzo Zarro is at the front looking at the camera. This was the last carrot washer sold by Carlo.

The Uccellini family, 1928: Frederick, Elizabeth, Gemma, Nafra, Carlo, Olga, and Louis.

The family 1928. Back row: Frederick, Gemma, Carlo, Louis.
Front row: Elizabeth, Nafra, and Olga.

In photographs that Carlo had arranged for (such as the car and family in front of the house (page 77), and the family photos on previous page), Carlo proudly displays the house, a growing family, a car and their farm he had built with his own hands. These pictures show that Carlo was realizing his dream: they had made it in America. These pictures were likely sent to Gemma's family in Italy to emphasize that point.

Note that in the family photos, both Louis and Frederick had pins on their jackets. When I asked Nafra about the pins, she said those were pins designed to celebrate Lindberg's flight over the Atlantic on May 20-21, 1927. According to Nafra, Carlo heard rumors that Lindberg was planning to take off from Roosevelt Field in Garden City, Long Island, New York and fly solo to Europe. During the buildup to the flight, Carlo went to Roosevelt Field every morning and waited hours before going back home convinced that it was too late for Lindbergh to start his flight. Finally on May 20, 1927, Carlo saw Lindberg emerge, and after some final preparations, he boarded the plane, taxied across the field and took off toward the northeast. Nafra did not convey what he thought of Lindberg's chances of making it, but Carlo came home that morning very excited about what he saw. Obviously he and the kids were proud of what Lindberg accomplished; as Carlo made sure the boys had their pins on for this picture. Nafra recalled the beginning of the airplane age in Central Park and then Bethpage, as aircraft flew over their house in those early days. An increasing number of those airplanes took off from a field along Central Avenue, which would later become the site of Grumman Aircraft. It was risky, as some airplanes crashed near town and one along Powell Avenue — crashes that made the news.

One can only imagine that Carlo's interest in the new transportation on wings, the airplane, which drew him to go to Roosevelt Field every morning to watch Lindberg take off. One also has to wonder if this interest was somehow passed along to his two sons, especially Frederick.

By all accounts, as the family entered the pre-depression era of the late 20's, they were a close, loving, industrious family who had a desire to learn, work and play. How the talents of Gemma and Carlo were passed down to their children will be described in the next chapter. Several stories passed along by Nafra and Dianne paint a picture of a close family who loved, enjoyed and respected their parents and each other.

Nafra once described to me one of Carlo's favorite pastimes of hiding candy around the house and in his room for his children to find. This is a trait my father carried with him, as he entertained his children and then his grandchildren, nieces and nephews, and even the neighborhood kids with candy he kept in the trunk of his car. Nafra also recounted to Dianne that "On Easter and Christmas my father would shop for chocolate candies Bunnies and eggs for Easter". Carlo also would buy Christmas motives for Christmas morning. "He would buy five of them, one for each child. Then on the big day he would take them and himself into the pantry alongside the kitchen, reach into the bag and say, 'who wants this one' until we each had one". Finally, Olga remembered that "On Sunday morning he'd give us a nickel and we would go to the candy store and get the most candy we could buy for a penny".

Another of Carlo's favorite activities was his enjoyment in taking his family on car rides. Olga recounted to Dianne: "On Sundays he always took the family out for a ride and always stopped at Jerk's to get an ice cream cone". "In winter he took us to the highest place on Long Island and we go sleigh riding down hill. What a walk coming back up".

But Carlo's favorite day trip involved taking his family to the beach. Most often the family went to Laurelton Beach at Laurel Hollow, Long Island (Near Cold Spring Harbor). From Dianne's notes of her conversation with Aunt Olga: "We use to pack a lunch and go to the beach early in the morning just to get a parking space as only about 30 cars could park near the beach. If you didn't get a space you had to park about 3 miles and hitch a ride or walk back."

Laurelton Beach is at the very end of a long windy road that passes the old Tiffany Estate. There are numerous family photos of the Uccellini family at Laurelton Beach. Going to the beach remained a tradition for the Uccellini family through the next 2 generations, a tradition that Louis, Nafra and Olga continued each summer taking their children to Laurelton, Oyster Bay and Jones Beach. But, Laurelton remained a favorite beach for my father's generation. Dianne recalls taking Nafra to that beach on several occasions as a place involving many family stories of Carlo, Gemma and their children. The very cold natural spring at the right side of the long winding dirt road was a harbinger that the beach was nearby. As Nafra aged, Dianne recalled several trips there, where they would enjoy the beauty, and reminisce. Much had changed. The road was now paved. The woods of trees were subdivided into lovely mini estates. Yet, the remnants of the old Tiffany Estate and the cold-water spring were still apparent as one approached the beach.

Louis and Nafra on Laurelton Beach.

Central Park, NY
Uccellini Family

1929

12 Schneider Lane, Central Park, NY
Nafra, Olga, Gemma & Libby Uccellini

Background is field between Nibbe Lane
and Powell Avenue School

Central Park, NY
Background is field between Corner of Broadway
and Powell Avenue from Schneider/Nibbe Lane

Nafra & Olga Uccellini **1928**

Central Park, NY
View from Nibbe Lane
across from Uccellini Property at
12 Schneider Lane, Central Park **1930**

Nafra Uccellini (Mulqueen)
with favorite doll
andBrownie the dog

Collection of photos, Central Park homestead.

Carlo , Gemma, Louis, Frederick, Elizabeth and Olga at Laurelton Beach.

Elizabeth, Nafra and Olga, 1939.

12: The children grow up; skills are passed down

Even as they worked the farm, the schooling of the children proceeded as both Carlo and Gemma insisted on a good education for the children. Furthermore, the skills and resourcefulness of the parents were being passed along to the children.

Sons Louis and Frederick worked with Carlo to help build the farm buildings, repair the farm equipment and work the farm(s). Louis proudly built a small storage barn, used to house the baby chicks. Later, this structure was moved closer to our house and became known as the "playhouse," which served as an outdoor getaway for all the children and was used to store our bikes during our childhood. I remember the playhouse fondly as a solidly built structure.

Louis would later become a foreman in Aircraft Specialties making his own jigs for the production of airplane parts used to build the Grumman fighter planes during World War II. Later in life, he would help his son Walter form a construction company in Troy, New York, where with Walter and his youngest son Thomas they would start up that company by building houses. The company would later emerge as a successful financial - construction - management company (United Group of Companies) under the leadership of Walter.

Frederick also helped to build the barns on the Central Park farm. But he took his engineering skills a step closer to Carlo as he expanded into "inventing" and building machines in his own right.   It seems Fred naturally picked up the mechanical talents and aviation interests of his father. As a teenager, he built a Ferris wheel, which was placed in the middle of Nibbe Lane, much to the annoyance of their neighbor across the street, James Amendola. Fred later became a key leader of Colonial Aircraft and the team that designed and built a seaplane called the "Skimmer," the first commercially available amphibian aircraft. He would eventually open up his own very successful manufacturing business in Greencastle, Pennsylvania.

Nafra, Olga, and Elizabeth all were taught homemaking skills from Gemma — skills and talents that Gemma brought over from Italy and were refined for prosperity in their new home in Central Park. These included raising chickens for eggs and meat (including killing and plucking them), preparing nourishing soups, cleaning, sewing, crocheting, gardening, and to be a positive helpmate to a husband. As the girls grew older, Gemma would sew their dresses from cloth from floral flour sacks. Gemma taught her daughters sewing, knitting and crocheting skills. Nafra and Olga became expert seamstresses, sewing dresses, shirts, tablecloths and costumes. But their mastery and pleasure was in sewing dresses and outfits for themselves and others as Nafra gained even more expert seamstress skills during the Depression while working in New York City in the garment industry. Nafra sewed almost all of her daughter Dianne's dresses from high school through college, 1955-1963. Nafra was so proficient a seamstress that Dianne was voted "Best Dressed" in high school. And while Dianne was in college, most all thought her outfits and formals were from high-end stores. In 1966 Nafra also sewed Dianne's crepe and lace wedding dress and her own lovely pink satin suit. In early adulthood, Olga sewed her outfits and formal gowns. Later she sewed dancing costumes for neighborhood children and dancing teachers and then for her daughter in the 1950s and 60s. In the 1970s, Olga sewed many exquisite dresses for her niece Calley, Nafra's granddaughter. Olga also sewed some of the gowns for the female attendants at her son's wedding and even made prom dresses

90

for their daughters and the girlfriends of their sons and nephews. These Uccellini women continued the excellent skills that Gemma passed down, beautiful and touching abilities. But Gemma was the Mistress of Crochet! No one could match Gemma's skill and dexterity.

**Frederick's ferris wheel on Nibbe Lane, 1929. Louis, sr. at top,
Olga or Elizabeth sharing the ride.**

**Kids Louis, Frederick, Nafra, Olga and Libby playing near the pumphouse
with Brownie the dog.**

1935

House seen from intersection of Nibbe and Schneider Lanes (looking East-Southeast). Barn in background.

13: The Depression

As with almost all Americans, the worldwide depression, which hit in the late 1920's and 1930's had a profound effect on the farming/immigrant community. Carlo and Gemma were no exceptions, although there is no evidence that they lost money in the Wall Street crash or the banking crisis that followed. Carlo continued to work his various jobs and was a productive farmer. But as was the case for many others during this period, he worked longer hours at reduced wages. Thus, Louis and Nafra quit school so they too could work where they could find it (again at reduced wages) and help at home. Nafra related to Dianne that she worked in the garment industry in New York City to help the family make ends meet. During the middle to late 30's, Fred also worked in the City at whatever jobs he could find. Elder Fred told his son Fred that the trip between New York City and Bethpage on the train could be frightening because there were many "tough guys on the way home, and they would attack and rob people for any money they had." What is remarkable is that even with the hardships that many suffered during the depression, the Uccellini family was amazingly resourceful and determined, as they did not seem to want for food, shelter or clothes. Carlo and Gemma always had a vegetable garden, vineyards and chickens and other animals for food. With Carlo and family members holding down many different jobs, Gemma and the girls making their own clothes and helping in the gardens, and the entire family saving their money, they seemed to have been able to get through the hardships and daily challenges that confronted much of the country during the Depression.

The Depression, and the related economic stress and stagnation, affected the entire globe, including Italy. During this period, Gemma continued her connections with her Italian family with an added incentive to help where she could, sending clothes and food to assist her brothers and sister. There are two letters written by Gino to Gemma during this period, one written in 1928 and one in 1938. Both letters point to an effort by Gino to buy Gemma's share of Cantalupo; probably motivated by the fact that Gemma had no intention of ever moving back to Italy. The 1938 letter indicates that Gemma had not yet signed the final documents to transfer her share of the family farm to her siblings, although stories told within the family as we were growing up indicates that she did sign sometime in the 1930's. The length of time between these two letters provides evidence that this must have been a difficult decision for Gemma. On one hand, Gemma was now set with her American family with no intention to return to her homeland and the sale would provide some money to the family still struggling with the Depression. On the other hand, her last tangible link to her home, the beautiful "hovel" that she left in December, 1913 would be broken forever. By 1938-39, she agreed, made this break with her Italian homeland and never looked back.

January 30, 1928

Dearest sister,

we just received your letter and we feel obliged to answer immediately, to clarify our own problems. I understand that you have been informed that we should inherit 150000 Lire. This, my dear Gemma, is an exageration for many reasons. Firstly, it is absolutely not true that the value of the property is what was stated, believe me, secondly, because of the atmosphere of crisis we have here in Italy, the value of the land as well as of the buildings has decreased substantially. I think that sister Annita has already written to you on this topic to tell you that we have found an agreement with her and we go along very well. Thus, in good agreement Anita is happy with the settlement of 5000 lire each. Cousins Aristodemo and Roberto were also involved. As for the payment, Annita (Lou, Annita sometimes is written with one n and sometimes 2 n's; I think Anita is right) has indicated that she is not requesting any payment this year, may be the following year. Now, please send us your power of attorney (Louis, this is a very liberal translation because I do not see how she could send fins a check!) and we would be grateful if you could leave the money with us for a little while, as you indicated in your last letter. This power of attorny should arrive here as soon as possible because the lawyer has told us that everything has to be completed by 25 February so that the deed can be done. I hope this letter will find you all in good health. We are all well. Best wishes to everyone. Kisses to the little nephews.   Your brother Gino.

First letter from Gino to Gemma, in regard to buying out Gemma's share of Cantalupo. English translation provided by Franco Enaudi.

Bargone 28/12/38

Dear sister

     I have not heard from you in a long time. I was very sad said not to have received news from you during the Christmas holidays. Our brother Savino has just come to visit me to find out if I have heard from you: I am writing to you in his presence. Your brothers here are all well and so are their families; we all hope that everything is well with you and your family and that your not writing is only due to the fact that your pen is lazy. Brother Savino, who is here with me as I mentioned, would like to know if you have received the last letter from the lawyer, which was supposed to be signed by the consul of the United States. I told you that the earlier letter was not sufficient since it was signed by the consul. I strongly urge you to write back right away and to send back immediately those documents that the lawyer sent you for the signature. We will reimburse you if the sending back of the documents is too costly. We need to build since the house is braced and in danger of falling down. But before we start the work we need to have completed all the necessary paper work with the village. Otherwise they will fine us. And the fine is not small. While waiting for a letter from you, we send you our best wishes for the New Year. We hope that the New Year will bring you and your family to Italy. Greetings to all of you from all of us. Your sister

Annita and Savino
Ferrari Savino
greetings from all of us

Second letter related to Gemma's share of Cantalupo, 1938.
English translation provided by Franco Enaudi.

1937

The main house on the Gardiner Farm, 1937.

14: The Gardiner Farm; Carlo is stricken by Parkinson's Disease

In 1935, Carlo and Gemma acquired a larger farm of over 200 acres in upstate New York near Gardiner, just west of the Hudson River in the southern Catskill region. The farm was purchased on March 3, 1935 through a land contract with Daniel D. Egan with a $3000 down payment, with several covenants, one stating that the parties of the second part (Carlo and Gemma) shall "quietly enjoy the said premises." Given the large sum of money needed for the down payment, one can only surmise if this came from savings; or perhaps from Gemma's share of the Cantalupo farm when she agreed to be bought out of her share by her Siblings in the late 1920's or the early 1930's.

The so-called Gardiner Farm still exists today and is located on the Albany Post Road outside of Gardiner, New York. It is not clear what Carlo's plan was for the farm, whether he planned to move the entire family up to this farm or whether he planned to rent it out and have it farmed accordingly. There are many family stories about how the boys, girls (now young men and women) and others worked hard to start the farm up. But there are no records as to whether any money was made or lost on the day-to-day operations of this farm.

The newly acquired Uccellini farm was located 2 farms down the road from a farm owned by the Mulqueen family. It was here that Nafra Uccellini met James Mulqueen and later married him on July 21, 1940. But this is the extent of the good news that came out of this experience in land/farm ownership, as tragedy struck in the 1937-1938 timeframe.

Shortly after purchasing the Gardiner Farm, Carlo became ill and progressively weaker over a relatively short period of time. By late 1937 or early 1938, Carlo was diagnosed with Parkinson's disease, a diagnosis that shocked and dismayed the family. Carlo's health rapidly deteriorated and his resolution began to fail. His inability to carry on with a large farm grew with each passing day. Given the location of the Gardiner Farm in upstate New York, hours away from their primary home in Bethpage, Long Island; Carlo became increasingly agitated as to how he would be able to sustain the larger Gardiner Farm in addition to the smaller farm in Bethpage. In 1938, Carlo decided that they would have to dispose of the Gardiner Farm, which they did on June 30, 1938, with the deed transferred to Victor E. McCord for just $1.00.

I heard stories when growing up that the upstate farm was basically let go "for taxes," that the agreement allowed Carlo and Gemma to avoid the upcoming tax bills on the Gardiner Farm and would also allow them to focus on sustaining the Bethpage homestead in the face of Carlo's growing weakness. Nafra stated during one of my last visits with her that for many years, family members spoke of their disappointment, bitterness and anguish over the decision to let the Gardiner Farm go. In a recent conversation, Fred Junior stated the same; that his father Frederick was quite bitter about the way the Gardiner Farm was sold for basically nothing. But the decision was made by Carlo, and from that point on his focus remained with the Bethpage homestead and his search for a cure that would rid him of the horrible disease that was overtaking his body.

Bethpage house at intersection of Nibbe Lane (left) and Schneider Lane (right), looking east-southeast (1941).

Louis D. Uccellini and Margaret A. Isemann on front stoop of Bethpage house, circa 1940.

15: The 1940's — Children marry; second generation children are born

In 1940, during the onset of World War II, Nafra married James Mulqueen whom she met during the period she helped at the Gardiner Farm. Jim was 30 years old. They had a daughter, Dianne born in 1941 and a son, Lenard born in 1943. They first lived in Walkill, NY, then on Cambridge Avenue, Bethpage. Later, after World War II, the Mulqueens moved in with Carlo and Gemma to assist them, before buying their own home on Central Boulevard in 1964.

In 1941, Louis married Margaret Isemann from Farmingdale, Long Island. They met in 1939 and then married in 1941. They had four sons; Charles, born 1942, Walter born 1945, Louis born 1949 and Thomas born 1950. They lived on Cambridge Avenue and on Lexington Avenue in Bethpage from 1949 to 1973, before moving to Troy, New York in 1973.

In 1943, daughter Olga married an Army Serviceman, Herbert Englehart, who was killed in action during the last days of World War II (see next chapter). Olga lived at home with her parents while Uncle Herbert was in the Service. On April 17, 1947, Olga's gave birth to a baby girl who she named Sheila. Olga married Henry Von Thaden in 1948. Henry was born in Germany but came to America as a young man and served in the US Army during the War, fighting fiercely in the Battle of the Bulge. They lived on Ellen Street in Bethpage just 6 blocks away from Carlo and Gemma, and had a son Henry John, born in 1952.

In 1944, Frederick married Emma Steiger. They had two sons, Frederick born in August 1945 and Robert born in 1947. They lived in Massapequa, Long Island about 5-10 miles from Bethpage before moving to Maine in the mid-1950s and then to Greencastle, Pennsylvania in the early 1960's.

In 1946, after World War II, Elizabeth married Clarence Durr and had a daughter Linda born in 1948. They lived in the Bronx, New York City, and drove approximately 1-1/2 hours almost each Sunday to visit the Long Island family.

Cousins, Sheila and Linda, enjoyed each other's company immensely. They were close in age, the daughters of twins Elizabeth and Olga and became very close friends as well as cousins. Linda says they used to pretend they also were "twins." They were the only younger girls in the second generation Uccellini family comprised of Dianne and the "Uccellini boys."

Starlight Fuel. Louis, Margaret and Dominich Demino, circa 1940.

Bethpage house looking northwest from the fields. Carlo, Louis, Gemma.

16: World War II

As World War II approached, and Fascist Italy was joining up with Germany as an enemy to the United States, Carlo and Gemma and their Italian-American compatriots were rocked by stresses associated with the mixed feelings of the political transition in Italy. How Gemma and Carlo felt about their homeland during the war is not entirely known. But their concerns had to be magnified as their own children were growing up, falling in love and getting married. Eugene Bellini made it clear to me (when we talked through a night in 1996 in Melbourne, Florida) as the War engulfing Europe and then the World made for great worry, that neither he nor anyone else amongst the close-knit Italian Bellini/ Uccellini families wanted to go over to fight a war in Europe, especially against Italy. But they all found themselves working in the rapidly expanding aircraft industry as the United States prepared for and entered the War.

Long Island had a number of aircraft manufacturing plants. Grumman Aircraft in Bethpage was a major Defense Contractor in the US that manufactured airplanes for the Navy, making the fighter planes that helped turn the Pacific war against Japan around. By late 1942-early 1943 Nafra's husband, Jim had obtained a job at Grumman and wound up working for Grumman for over 30 years as an inspector. Carlo's son, Frederick also worked for Grumman.

Through a family connection on Margaret Uccellini's side of the family (a lawyer named Mr. Hogan), Louis got a job at Aircraft Specialties in Hicksville, New York that was a subcontractor to Grumman Aircraft. Louis was able to get Eugene Bellini a job at Aircraft Specialties as well and both rose within the ranks, with Louis becoming the principle shop foreman. Working for the war industry and having children made them eligible for deferments. As such, Carlo and Gemma's sons and son in law (Jim) qualified for deferments that allowed them to contribute to the American war effort in a meaningful way.

Olga's husband Herbert Englehart, who was living in Reading, Pennsylvania when inducted, and in the Army when he met Olga, was the only member of the extended family that was at risk during WWII. Herbert was stationed on Long Island when he and Olga met in early 1943. They were married December 12, 1943. As Dianne recalls, everyone in the family liked him. He was a gentlemanly person, a good man. He was assigned to the Army Engineer Battalion Corps and was dispatched to the Pacific Theatre in early 1945. Tragically, he was killed on April 2, 1945 in the Sea of Okinawa by a Kamikaze pilot. Herbert was on deck of a ship when the Kamikaze hit the ship. He was buried at sea.

april 11. 1943

Herbert Englehart, April 19, 1943.

This photo was taken in mid-1943, while Olga and Herbie were courting.

December 12, 1943 Marriage of Olga Uccellini and Herbert Englehart.
Olga's siblings Elizabeth and Fred Uccellini were maid of honor and best man.

Dianne and Uncle Herbie. Photo taken at Uccellini kitchen entrance.

Not much was ever said about Uncle Herbert while the next generation grew up. I only recall being told once or twice about him by my mother and Uncle Jim, with an emphasis about how he died. The memory of Herbert is provided mostly by Dianne, the oldest grandchild, who fondly recalls his caring and thoughtful conversations with her. She also recalls the day that the shocking and heart breaking news that he was killed in action and buried at sea as it was delivered to Olga and the rest of the family. Grief and tears overwhelmed everyone.

By any measure, of all the children, Olga experienced the greatest impact and most tragic personal loss from World War II. Nevertheless, by the 1946-1947 timeframe, the focus of the entire family was turning to the continued deterioration of Carlo as he battled the ravages of the Parkinson's disease. The battle continued unabated through the 1940's and would eventually lead to his death in 1950.

Carlo holding hands with first and second grandchildren: Dianne Mulqueen and Charles Uccellini outside the Bethpage home, 1943.

17: Carlo's death; Gemma's grief

His painful fight against the ravages brought on by Parkinson's disease dominated the last decade of Carlo's life. The best way to visually document Carlo's deterioration is by the sequence of pictures below, taken between 1940 and 1946. The 1940 wedding picture of James Mulqueen to Nafra shows that rigidity/stiffness related to Parkinson's disease was already afflicting Carlo. The 1943 picture of Carlo with Louis holding Charles, Carlo's mother Maria, and Gemma shows a thinner Carlo who was more rigid. The 1946 photo illustrates how the disease continued to weaken Carlo, with the haunting, gaunt look clearly evident in the wedding picture of Clarence Durr to Elizabeth. During this period, as Carlo became sicker and weakened by this disease, the entire family remained perplexed on how he could have been afflicted with such a disease with no family history anyone knew of.

Carlo's daughter, Nafra's wedding to James Mulqueen July 21,1940. L to R: Bill Mulqueen, Olga, Gemma, James, Nafra and Carlo.

The family rallied to provide whatever support they could for Carlo and Gemma. Jim Mulqueen's new job at Grumman led them to move from Walkill, New York to Cambridge Avenue in Bethpage, a new neighborhood consisting of simple homes built to house many of the defense contract workers for Grumman Aircraft as they ramped up during World War II. Their Cambridge Avenue house was just a few blocks from the Uccellini farm, enabling Nafra to be closer to Carlo and Gemma to provide help that was becoming an urgent need. During the 1940's, Carlo sought out many new treatments to fight off the effects of Parkinson's disease and often traveled to New York City by the Long Island Railroad in response to new claims, only to be disappointed repeatedly. And he continued to weaken. By 1946 or 1947 Nafra, Jim, Dianne and Lenard moved from their Cambridge Avenue home back to Carlo and Gemma's house on Schneider Lane so Nafra could help Gemma provide for the immediate care of Carlo.

Louis holding Charles, Maria Rastelli (Carlo's mother), Carlo and Gemma. Late 1942.

February wedding of daughter, Elizabeth Uccellini to Clarence Durr.
Gemma, Carlo, Elizabeth and Clarence. Photo taken in Uccellini living room.

During and after the War, Louis and Margaret also rented a house on Cambridge Avenue, across the street from Nafra and Jim and next to the Bellini's. In 1947 to 1948 timeframe, Louis and his wife, Margaret, were deeded land on the northeast corner of the farm (corner of Nibbe Lane and Lexington Avenue), and moved a house (a model home from what was the lumber mill down the street) to the 26 Lexington Avenue address where they raised their growing family of four boys.

From there, Louis trekked down to Carlo's house every night to help Nafra care for their father. Dianne vividly remembers Carlo calling out with a mournful cry: "Gemma,"… "Gemma." Gemma at times just did not have the mental nor physical strength to respond, which just increased Carlo's anguish. She sat down in the basement and listened to the call, trapped like Carlo by this insidious disease that slowly worked its death march on the human body. By the late 1940's her husband's body turned to a weakened mass unable even to shuffle across the floor. Louis and Frederick would have to carry their father to the bathroom and to the bathtub and back to his bed; and he would always call with an increasingly slurred speech for Gemma to help him with a mournful cry: "Gemma," … "Gemma," … "Gemma."

Toward the end, Carlo developed an infection that required an increasing number of trips to the hospital. But Carlo did not go down quietly, as recounted to me by Uncle Jim and also my mother. During his last days, Carlo was brought to a hospital where Gemma and the rest of the family could watch over him. At some point, Gemma knew the end was near and thought Carlo was unconscious. Though Gemma knew that Carlo harbored very strong feelings against the Catholic Church, she remained committed to the church and believed he needed to have the Last Rites ministered. Gemma called in a priest to administer the Last Rites, during which time Carlo emerged from his apparent unconscious state. He realized what was going on; and at that moment he loudly and unequivocally renounced the Catholic Church, the priest and the Last Rites. The priest left. Gemma collapsed into a chair sobbing quietly in uncontrolled grief. Shortly thereafter, Carlo died peacefully on January 7, 1950.

Dianne recalls that the women in the family were all crying. Dianne also started to cry, and she recounts that Nanny went over to her and said quietly, "Don't cry. We're alright. Grandpa is not hurting anymore. We're sad he's gone."

My brother, Walter, told me a story after my father, Louis died on April 3, 1989. He said that when my father heard that his father Carlo had died, he sat on his bed at home and cried uncontrollably with his head bowed and buried in his hands. It was the only time Walter said he saw our father cry. My father never told me anything about his father's death and I never saw him cry, ever.

Because Carlo renounced the priest, his Last Rites and the Catholic Church while on his deathbed, the issue of where to bury him suddenly emerged. Carlo and Gemma had secured gravesites at St. Mary's Cemetery, but the Church disallowed his burial there. The family located a plot and buried Carlo at the Amityville Cemetery, Harrison Avenue, Amityville, New York. A plot was also secured for Gemma for when her time came.

Nanny with Louis William Uccellini on April 16, 1950, his first birthday. Picture taken in kitchen of Louis and Margaret's house less than 3 months after Carlo's death.

18: Gemma refocuses on the family

Gemma's life during Carlo's long battle against Parkinson's disease became increasingly burdened by the need to care for Carlo on a continuous basis and to deal with the effects of this disease on Carlo and on the surrounding family. As Gemma increasingly focused on, and became overwhelmed by, the crisis surrounding Carlo's deteriorating health, she became more detached to others and more distant to her grandchildren.

With Carlo's death in January of 1950, Gemma must have felt the burden lift, even as she grieved for her lost husband. She started to emerge from her grief and began to focus her attention on the two youngest grandchildren who lived close by: Sheila (now 3 years old) and (me), Louis (now 1 year old). Sheila and I did not know of the trauma that surrounded Carlo's death. We simply demanded Gemma's (always known to us as Nanny) time and attention. Nanny reciprocated, with attention and affection. Although she focused on the two younger grandchildren, she also seemed to me to be enlightened and interested in all of her grandchildren and especially our education, saying over and over again to me and others: "you must save your money" and "you must go to college." And she always was interested in our friends, especially our girl and boy friends, when we got to that age.

For the first time since her marriage, Nanny had "free time." As Dianne recalls, she indulged her love of gardening, especially tending the many rows of peonies she had planted in the side yard, years prior. She also took pleasure and pride in her red roses planted in the front and back yard. The sweet smelling wild white roses were an integral part of the border of bushes planted along Nibbe Lane, near the front of the house. The cherry trees in the back were still producing prolifically. She'd gather up the men and boys in her family to help her pick the cherries when they were in season.

By approximately 1953 or so the house had been divided into apartments. Apparently this was done to provide some financial stability to sustain Nanny and allow her to keep the property. The original back of the house: side entrance, kitchen, dining room, and pantry were converted into an apartment on the ground floor to rent out. The original ground floor sewing room was converted into a kitchen/sitting room. The original living room became her bedroom. With Nafra's family living upstairs, she'd used that bathroom. In the mornings she would have the radio on, set to an Italian station. Italian music and opera could be heard coming from her bedroom. As Dianne recalls, hearing it was comforting yet quaint, an assurance that Nanny had maintained her interests in Italian news and culture in addition to caring for her family.

Nanny's weekly traditions included excursions to the Farmers' Market on the border between Bethpage and Hicksville. My father would drive Nanny to the Farmers' Market, often accompanied by me, Tommy and his nieces Sheila and Linda. We all have our memories of the Saturday mornings at Farmers' Market, the merchants and how Nanny would always taste the Parmagiano and Reggiano cheese, feel the fruit, sample the meat prior to purchasing.

Nanny was also a companion with her grown children and grandchildren on long family trips and related vacations. In 1951 or 1952 she went with the Nafra, Jim and Dianne to Niagara Falls and Watkins Glen. She often went to Maine as family members visited Uncle Fred and Aunt Emma (and

112

cousin Fred and Robert) during the summer. In 1965, she went with Louis and Margaret (and me and Tom) to Jackson, Mississippi to visit Margaret's sister Ada and her family; a trip made during the hottest time of the year (July) in a car without any air conditioner.

Nanny and Dianne on a trip to upstate New York, standing before Niagara Falls.

Gemma and Sheila on a trip to upstate New York.

Nafra and Gemma overlooking Niagara Falls.

Nanny knew how to preserve some of her family cooking traditions. Nanny's cooking of the Italian soups (Pasta Rassa and Angulange (Unulaine) was legendary, a special treat for Christmas and Easter meals. Nanny's preparation of those meals became a ritual and tradition each year. Angulange is like small ravioli filled which rich meat that is cooked in a beef/chicken broth. As recalled by Dianne, Nafra and Nanny would prepare the meat ingredients the day before: shopping, chopping, cooking and grinding. The next day Nanny would prepare the pasta. She'd make a large well of flour, insert a dozen eggs and some salt and then knead, knead, knead. She would roll the pasta on a large table size wooden board with a long 3-foot wooden roller. Until you have tried this, you have no idea the strength Nanny had. Nafra, Olga, Elizabeth, Margaret and Dianne then prepared for the assembly line. The dollops of meat would be dropped in a line interspersed on the pasta, then the pasta rolled over and pinched, cut off and stored. Then the next row would be filled pinched off and cut, and the next. Usually about 250-400 ravioli were made. Because no one had a freezer to hold so many of the Unulaine, they would store the individual ravioli covered on a board in the "sun room." During winter this room was unheated so it was the perfect place to store them until the families were ready to pick up their share. And always the Unulaine was anticipated and enjoyed with gusto.

And finally there were the simple, day-to-day family get-togethers. It seemed that every evening my father would either visit Nanny, Nafra and Jim, or Nanny would walk down the trail between her house and our house on Lexington Avenue, a trail that cut between the barn and chicken coop and past the Playhouse, where our dog King was chained, and then to our back door. Up until 2013, the indentation along that trail was still visible in the smaller backyard of Carlo and Gemma's house, now owned by Lenard and Laura Mulqueen — an indentation that pointed to the family ties that were maintained over this period. Alas, recent landscaping finally eliminated the last vestiges of this trail.

The trail leading from the back of Gemma and Carlo's house, past the barn and chicken coop to Louis and Margaret's house. The dog King and Charlie also visible in background. Picture taken in August 1957.

Louis Uccellini near the trail leading from the back of Gemma and Carlo's house, past the barn and chicken coop to Louis and Margaret's house, early 1960's.

116

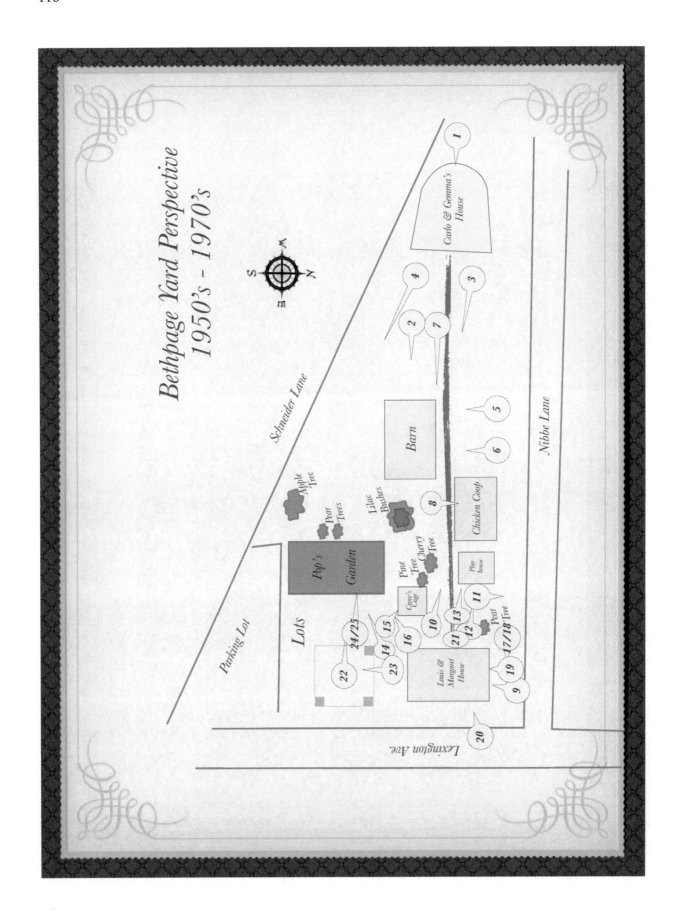

19: Nanny preserves the Bethpage farm

Nanny made an important decision that was to shape the lives of all her grandchildren. Nanny decided to keep the Bethpage farm intact and refused to sell any of the land. This one act had enormous consequences for the grandchildren and represented the victory lap for Carlo and Gemma's lifetime journey to America.

She kept the barn, the chicken coop, the beloved playhouse, the lots, vegetable garden, fruit trees, flower beds, everything; kept it all together "to let the grandchildren play in." Her decision to keep the farm intact made it the largest yard in Bethpage for miles. By preserving this farm, the buildings and the lots for us to have all to ourselves gave the next generation confidence to move forward and explore, provided us a sense of control and an ability to organize the daily activities without hovering parental supervision and instilled a sense of purpose that carried us forward in many ways.

And this dream world, preserved by Nanny's decision was ours, all ours, with our rules. The farm became our world where cars could be rebuilt, all kinds of games played all year round (baseball, football, Ringalevio, hide and seek, archery, camping out, playing "guns," collecting all kinds of animals in "zoos"), where you could raise the talking "Joe the Crow" in a huge cage under a growing pine, have cookouts, play croquet, hold knock hockey tournaments, play badminton, sneak girls into the barn thinking that the moms really did not know what was going on, and just hang out, eating cherries, pears and apples right off the trees and camp overnight and cook breakfast outdoors the following morning.

There are, of course, many more fond memories:

— My father's (Pop's) garden with sweet corn, tomatoes, lettuce, pumpkins and countless other vegetables.

— The large circle of lilacs near the barn that bloomed in June and served as home base for Ringalevio.

— Cookouts on the far back yard of roasted cooked potatoes, fresh corn, tomatoes with family and friends.

— Walter building go-karts with old lawnmower engines; Charlie, Lenny, friends rebuilding their hotrods.

— Uncle Fred, cousins Fred and Robert arriving just as the cherries ripened, to climb the trees, pick and eat.

— Charlie falling from the apple tree and breaking his arm!

— Going up into the upper barn to look over the "treasures," the stored furniture of whom?

— The many baseball and football games played in the lots complete with an opening day ceremony for the baseball and football season.

— Uncle Jimmy's immaculate lawn between the house and the barn.

— Tracking through the drifts and deep snow from the many childhood snowstorms, with the drifts and forts constructed from snow blocks providing cover during the intense snowball fights which followed.

This one deliberate decision by Nanny provided confidence-building experiences, and indeed a foundation that carried the grandchildren forward in many ways, and provided the fond memories that will live with us for the rest of our lives.

The total experience offered by this world, this opportunity provided by Nanny, shaped the lives of the next generation of children that Carlo and Gemma really lived for, for whom they gave up Italy for when they decided to make their journey to America.

1. Dianne, Sheila, Freddy and Linda, in front of Bethpage house, 1954.

2. Lenny, Sheila and Linda, early 1950's. Looking southeast towards barn.

3. Feb. 1961 snowscape from backdoor.

4. Feb. 1961 snowscape looking SE from house.

5. The barn, January 1970.

6. The barn, January 1970.

7. Lenny on Uncle Jim's lawn.

9. Louis, sr. and the 4 boys -- Charlie, Louis, Tommy and Walter, 1951.

8. Walter feeding chickens by the coop.

10. Tommy in snow with cherry tree and barn in background. March 1956.

11. Tommy, Louis and King.

14. Louis sr. and Walter with crow. Garden in background.

12. January 1955. Louis, Charlie, Walter and Tommy with King.

15. Joe the crow, backyard.

13. King, cherry tree and barn in background.

16. Sheila, Louis and Louis sr. with the crow, 1959. Garden and Kessler's factory in background.

17. Louis and Walter, croquet sideyard.

20. House at 26 Lexington Avenue

18. Sideyard, Louis Agiesta, Tommy, Sal Carbo, Henry with King. 1962.

21. Louis sr. at back door of Lexington Ave. house.

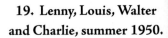

19. Lenny, Louis, Walter and Charlie, summer 1950.

123

22. Football Saturday. Tommy, Louis, Henry with lots, fort and barn in background.

24. Pumpkin harvest. Tommy and Henry with barn in background.

23. Walter and his go-kart.

25. Pumpkin harvest. Tommy, Walter, King, Louis sr. and Louis. Fall 1957.

Gemma, her sister Anita and Mrs. Emma DeLalio in Italy, 1964.

20: 1964: Nafra and Jim purchase their own home; Nanny visits Italy

There were four events during the 60's; the first two unsettled Gemma and the third and fourth rocked us all to the core. In early 1964, Nafra and Jim decided to purchase their own house after many years of living in Nanny's house, caring for Carlo and Gemma, and making many sacrifices along the way. With an obvious sense of disappointment that Nafra and Jim wanted to leave her house for one of their own, Nanny decided she wanted to stay in her house and live alone, which she did. This split was an unsettling one for the family for reasons not really understood by the grandchildren, even though it seemed more than natural that Nafra and Jim would want their own home after sacrificing themselves in the care for Carlo and Gemma for so many years. Nevertheless, the tension between Nafra and Gemma existed (just below the surface) for the next 2 years.

Then in the summer of 1964, Gemma returned to Italy to much fanfare in the local press (returning after 50 years). While she was grateful to see her brothers and sister, she seemed disappointed upon her return; perhaps the old tensions between her and her sister Anita emerged during this reunion. Even though Lenard was able to be with her during portions of that trip back to her Italian home, Gemma was somewhat unsettled by the visit with a sister who was still smarting from the failure of her plot to keep Gemma separated from Carlo those 50 years prior to Gemma's return to Italy. Gemma also wondered why she sacrificed to send clothes and food over to Anita when they now seemed to have it all. And although she really missed Anita, Gino and Savino after returning to America, she knew she would not be going back to Italy again.

Gemma, with Anita (kneeling in front) in Salsomaggiore, Italy 1964 with Anita's family and Lenard Mulqueen (Gemma's grandson) second from right.

Gemma with Anita and family members in Salsomaggiore, Italy, 1964.

Gemma with Anita (left) and Gino (right) in front of church in Italy, 1964. (likely Fidenza).

Gemma, in front of Cantalupo house with Anita (left) and family members, 1964.

Gemma in Italy, 1964 (likely at Cantalupo).

21: Sheila

As noted earlier, Gemma was a special Nanny to Sheila and me for reasons related to us being the youngest grandchildren that lived very close to her when Carlo died in 1950. The closeness which developed between Nanny and Sheila and me helped to forge a closeness between Sheila and me which carried us through our childhood into high school, calling each other "cuz" wherever and whenever. In the Fall of 1964 when I broke my leg playing football as a sophomore in high school and was on crutches for 8 weeks, Sheila immediately volunteered to carry my books between many of the classes. But it just wasn't me. Sheila seemed special to all of us, she could simply light up the room with her beauty, charm and kindness, bringing cheer to those around her. In June of 1965, Sheila graduated from Bethpage High School and was noticeably in love with her high school sweetheart, Michael Picucci. By early fall of that year, there was talk that they were going to marry each other, which to me seemed perfectly fine despite their young age.

Sheila was a baton twirler in high school.   **Freddy, Linda, Sheila and Robert, 1963.**

In November 1965 after Sheila had complained of a nagging and increasing pain in her right leg, she was diagnosed with a rare bone cancer in her knee. Upon the initial diagnosis of her cancer on November 9, 1965, my father came home from work in the late morning and drove Sheila, Michael, Aunt Olga and Uncle Henry to a special cancer hospital in New York City. November 9, 1965 is also the same day through night that New York City, much of the Northeast and Quebec Canada suffered a total electrical blackout due to an operator induced system error in the electric grid, which all started in Quebec. By 5:30pm, New York City and Long Island were plunged into darkness.

And so that evening, as we waited for my father to return from New York City, I clearly remember sitting in the dark living room of our house with my mother and brother Tommy with two candles offering a flickering light as we all tried to comprehend how something like this could happen to Sheila. When my father did return later that night after a harrowing and silent drive home, he told us the horrible diagnosis as we sat in the darkness, that the cancer was in the knee and leg bones and that they would have to amputate Sheila's leg just above the knee to save her life. He then sat there for a while and when we ran out of questions that must of just added to his grief, he got up, walked through the darkness into his room and closed the door.

After the operation, Sheila seemed to be making a remarkable recovery. She spoke of the phantom pains that made her think she still had her leg and foot, but these did not seem to faze her. She got fitted for prosthesis and set upon learning to walk again. And with a goal to walk down the aisle, Michael Picucci and Sheila got engaged to be married. Although just 19 years old, they decided to get married in the spring of 1966 as Sheila continued to recover from the cancer and related amputation.

Sheila was a beautiful bride as she walked down the aisle arm in arm with Uncle Henry to her waiting husband. Tragically, the happiness of that day did not last long. Shortly after the wedding, symptoms related to the cancer reemerged. Sheila was quickly overwhelmed by the ravages of the cancer spreading throughout her body. By late spring and early summer, it became clear to us that she was not going to make it. Sheila died a painful death in August of 1966, a death that put her at peace, but which devastated the family; the trauma of what was happening leaving a hole in every heart.

All of us to some extent were never the same after witnessing Sheila's losing fight against this cancer. Gemma's grief and sense of loss was overwhelming and intense. She often asked very quietly, but firmly, why God took Sheila and why God did not take her. Nafra, Aunt Libby, my father Louis and other family aunts and uncles were visibly shaken to the core. But the impact on Olga was immense, a crushing blow that would only abate slowly over time. Olga was devastated, as any mother would be and was never the same. Her laughter seemed to cease. She became less engaged with her larger family and detached from her previous total immersion and joy in life.

Michael Picucci, who has become a well-known psychologist with a focus on spiritual and physical healing from traumatic losses, wrote in his book *"The Journey Toward Complete Recovery"* (1996) about the impact on him during Sheila's battle against the cancer that took her life. On the next page is an excerpt from his book about that loss and his struggles. Michael's words provide a clear recognition of how important Sheila was to our lives and how important it is for us to realize how painfully devastating this traumatic event was to her, her immediate family, and to all of us who shared her life.

Quoting Michael Picucci, from his book *"The Journey Toward Complete Recovery"* (1996):

Some of the complex feelings involved in grief work are sadness, anger, remorse, hurt, depression and loneliness. The duration depends on the severity of the loss, and the degree to which it may trigger other unconscious losses.

In my own grief work, I was amazed at the intensity and depth surrounding those emotionally forgotten patches of my history. The first trauma surfaced when I was 32 years old and newly abstinent from drugs and alcohol. What erupted in me was the complex feelings of loss and grief surrounding the death of my teenage bride eleven years earlier.

We had married young. I was age eighteen. It was one of those wonderful and crazy teenage things, a time of great learning and great confusion. Sheila and I were aware of all of our immature traits, but our love and commitment were unquestionable. In the three years that we had together, Sheila suffered a leg amputation from a rare bone cancer, which later metastasized to her lung. She died after a year of tortuous physical, psychic and emotional pain.

She died without us ever having acknowledged that she had a terminal disease or discussing her impending death. Times were different then: we did not know how to negotiate such complexities. This emotional incompleteness caused me much pain. I had somehow shrouded the entire trauma.

In therapy, eleven years later, the entire experience unraveled. With deep feeling I rediscovered and shared many of the pains and confusions from the compounded traumas, as well as many of the sweet and tender moments that counterbalanced them. I remembered the day at the hospital when the doctor informed me that her leg would have to be amputated. It was the night of the East Coast electrical blackout. It took six hours to drive home with her mother, neither of us saying a word. The setting was strangely appropriate: My whole world was going dark but I didn't know how or where, to express my feelings. As I finally came out of my own "blackout" I recalled the struggles my wife endured when she was fitted for prosthesis and had to learn to walk again, I remembered the coughing spells that signaled her pneumonia.

When all of this came back to me, my foremost emotion was shame. I was ashamed of my emotional incompleteness. I felt that I could have comforted us both more if only I had known how to communicate effectively. I felt I failed her. I was ashamed of the helplessness that I felt throughout the entire crisis. My complex thoughts and feelings of relief when she finally died compounded this shame.

In therapy, after experiencing my emotions, I was able to reconnect with the love and tenderness of our union. This came over me like a wave of peace. It felt as though the best and most loving parts of my deceased partner instantly surrounded and engulfed me. In the purity and amplification of these feelings, my soul was restored. I immediately felt more open and more alive. Love lived in my heart again. When I shared all of these feelings, I gained the ability to once again have a significant, loving relationship.

Marriage of Sheila Von Thaden to Michael Picucci in Spring, 1966.

```
                    IN MEMORY OF SHEILA

In 1963, at the time I gradudated college and left home for San Francisco, I had a
photo album in which I included photos of family including Sheila.  Next to each
photo I wrote a caption or copied a meaningful quotation.  Because of the special
affection I felt for Sheila, who was more like a "little sister" and a joyous ray of
sunshine, I had placed the following quotation next to her photo.

                    "When I have gone away
                    and said farewell to home
                    And left my house empty,

                    O plum-tree beside my roof
                    don't forget to bloom
                    each spring."

Somehow, I felt she was "HOME" ...she represented the spirit of care, joy, love and
renewal I felt for my large family, my roots, and my home that I had left.    ...
She was my plum tree... to bloom each spring.

Sheila was a gift to us.  She was with us only a short time.  She went before us to
our larger HOME, and I have missed her.

At my former home in San Jose and this one also, I've planted plum trees.

The delicate pink blossoms, exquisite, and fragile, exhibit a serene joy when they
arrive.  Their deep wine colored leaves provide a lovely, significant contrast,  a
complement and focal point to the landscape and my home.  They have provided me an
abiding beauty and assuredness.

                    ...And they bloom again each Spring.
```

From Dianne Mulqueen Sullivan.

As is sometimes the case, a tragic loss acts to bridge a gulf within a family. After Sheila's funeral and burial, we all gathered at Nafra and Jim's house to mourn Sheila's loss, celebrate her life and support each other. Either my father or Nafra/Jim drove Nanny from the cemetery and to Nafra's house. For the first time, Nanny stepped inside Nafra and Jim's house and joined the family for this somber occasion. Sheila's life, and now her death, served to change Gemma's life at times of tragic loss, this time bringing Gemma and Nafra back together. In their shared grief over the loss of Sheila, the mother-daughter bond was reestablished, never to be broken for the rest of their lives. And while we weep for Sheila and for what might have been, we must celebrate her life, as short as it was. She deserves nothing less.

As if the tragedy of losing Sheila was not enough, Uncle Clarence, Elizabeth's husband, died 2 weeks later. His daughter, Linda was only 18. Linda had lost her father and her favorite cousin in the same month.

134

Gemma with her children, Nafra, Olga, Libby, Louis and Fred. Taken August 1977.

22: The End of the Journey

Nanny was clearly shaken to the core with Sheila's death in 1966. No one can imagine the depths of her pain. She had cared for and loved Sheila since she was born. She seemed traumatized but like all of us, she too internalized her grief and attempted to move on. Dealing with her grief was helped by arrival of the next generation at her house in 1966 of her first great grandson to watch over. Walter and Sheila Ryan Mullen married in January 1966. With their newborn son, Michael, they moved into Nanny's house and lived there for over a year while Walter readied himself to go back to RPI in Troy, New York to finish his college education. Having Michael in the house at this time was a godsend for Nanny who could focus on her first great grandson in a time of grief, as she did with Sheila and me after Carlo died in 1950. Michael became the favorite for all, not only Nanny, but also for his uncles and grandparents Louis and Margaret. The young couple and their child living with Nanny was exactly what were needed to help Nanny recover from Sheila's death.

But the world around Nanny, defined by the closeness of her grandchildren, was rapidly changing. Dianne married Bob Sullivan in 1966 and decided to stay in California. In 1967, Charlie and Vivian Crepes married and moved out to Islip, Long Island. Walter, Sheila and Michael moved up to Troy in 1967. And Louis left for his first year of college in Syracuse, New York that same year. Tommy left for college (WPI) in 1969. Lenard married Laura Nash on February 22, 1970. Lenard and Dianne were starting their own lives away from Nanny's home that they grew up in.

The grandchildren were leaving the farm. The world that Nanny had preserved was getting quiet and empty of the children that were always around, until now.

In September 1970, Nanny suffered a massive stroke in the upstairs portion of her home. The stroke seemed relatively mild at first. Nafra, who visited Nanny every day, discovered Nanny on the floor in her upstairs portion of the house and called the doctor who unfortunately decided to keep her home under observation. Within 24 hours, Nanny fell into an unconscious state. And worse, the right side of body became paralyzed. After several weeks in a nursing home where Nanny slowly regained her consciousness, it became readily apparent that she had trouble communicating. Although Nanny seemed to understand when people spoke to her in English, she only could speak in her Italian dialect.

Nafra decided (on the spot in the nursing home) that she was going to take her mother home to care for her. What no one realized at the time was that Nanny would live another 9 and half years. Like Carlo, Nanny was trapped in a body that could not fully respond making her dependent on the day to day care for almost ten years. She needed the constant assistance of the family around her, a massive effort that fell mostly to Nafra and Jim. Nanny would need Nafra's help to get in and out of the wheelchair that became her home within the house. Nafra had to assist Nanny to get dressed, to cook for her, to bathe her and to use the bathroom. Nanny taught herself to use her left hand side to feed herself. Through all of this, Nanny always maintained a positive spirit, while Nafra and Jim were always there to meet her needs.

As Nafra, Jim and others cared for Nanny after her stroke, the world Gemma and Carlo created and preserved was changing. In June 1971, I graduated from the University of Wisconsin-Madison with a degree in Meteorology and married Susan Eichman. After the wedding ceremony, we drove back east to celebrate our marriage with our family at the Bethpage homestead with those family members who couldn't make it to the wedding in Madison. During the party and cookout, my father brought Nanny from Nafra's house to our home to celebrate our wedding with the rest of the family. The picture below shows Nanny in a wheel chair and my father all smiles as we cut the wedding cake. This photo is taken near the same spot in the Bethpage kitchen where the photo on page 110 was taken 21 years earlier. As far as I know, this was the last time Nanny was brought back to the farm she still owned.

Louis and Susan Uccellini in Bethpage kitchen for wedding party in June 1971.
Louis sr. and Gemma in background.

After our short visit back home, Susie and I returned to Madison where I would pursue graduate degrees in Meteorology over the next 6 years. Thomas was attending Worcester Polytechnic Institute in Massachusetts. Louis and Margaret Uccellini were setting new sights in their move to Troy, New York where Louis would soon join Walter in the startup of a real estate and construction business.

In July 1972, the Uccellini farmland was sold. This sale included the barn, chicken coop and the playhouse along with the entire lots, garden and treed areas that served as the playground for our youth. Lenard and Laura bought the house that Carlo built on Nibbe Lane, with the purchase including a small amount of the original farmland immediately behind the house.

On August 14, 1972, the day after Thomas Uccellini married Janet Amendola and moved to Worcester, Massachusetts, the bulldozers appeared and proceeded to knock down the farm buildings, taking out the splendid Playhouse and chicken coop with one slice. The farmland was cleared for three houses. The paradise that Nanny had preserved while the grandchildren were growing up, the stage upon which we discovered the world, was gone forever.

DIRECTIVE

"Back out of all this now too much for us,
Back in time made simple by the loss
Of detail, burned, dissolved, and broken off
Like graveyard marble sculpture in the weather,
There is a house that is no more a house
Upon a farm that is no more a farm….
First there's the children's house of make-believe,
Some shattered dishes underneath a pine,
The playthings in the playhouse of the children.
Weep for what little things could make them glad…."
—Robert Frost

Nanny was aware of the decision to sell the property, but was of course separated from what had to be done. She never returned to the house that Carlo built nor did she see the changes brought on by the sale of the farm. Settled into the routine of care provided to her by Nafra and Jim, she seemed to enjoy how all the grandchildren would bring their new husband or wife to her and relished seeing the new great grandchildren that seemed to come along in waves during the 1970's. But she also was extremely frustrated when she could not talk to anyone in English, and Nafra would have to stop what she was doing to translate for her. Nanny would want to show Louis' new wife Susan how to crochet and/or knit. Nanny was always a good teacher with much patience, but with the paralysis and aphasia, it was very difficult. If Susan was making a mistake that a stitch would need to be taken out and redone sooner rather than later, Nanny would become totally frustrated by her paralysis and inability to tell Susan in English what needed to be done to fix the problem (again necessitating a call to Nafra).

As the years went by and she outlived her favorite brother in law (Uncle Frank), Nanny talked more often of the burden she was putting on Nafra and Jim. In the late 1970's and especially 1979, Nanny weakened noticeably and had at harder time eating. During my Christmas visit in 1979, she looked me right in the eye when I was leaving to go back to Maryland with Susan and our first child, Anthony, and held my hand tight with her left hand and said in English "Good bye."

In January 1980, Gemma was taken to the hospital where she was treated for a blocked bowel. She decided there that she wanted to go home and die in peace. After returning home and after becoming less responsive to those around her, she was ministered her Last Rites by a Catholic priest.

On January 11, 1980, nine and half years after the stroke that confined her to a wheelchair, Gemma died peacefully in her sleep. Gemma was buried next to Carlo in the Amityville Cemetery.

Gemma Ferrari Uccellini's journey was over.

THE SIMPLE GRAVESTONES FOR GEMMA AND CARLO.

LOOKING FOR A
SUNSET BIRD IN WINTER

The West was getting out of Gold,
The breath of air had died of cold,
When shoeing home across the white,
I thought I saw a bird alight.

In summer when I passed the place,
I had to stop and lift my face;
A bird with an angelic gift
Was singing in it sweet and swift.

No bird was singing in it now.
A single leaf was on a bough,
And that was all there was to see
In going twice around the tree.

From my advantage on a hill
I judge that such a crystal chill
Was only adding frost to snow
As gilt to gold that wouldn't show.

A brush had left a crooked stroke
Of what was either cloud or smoke
From north to south across the blue;
A piercing little star was through.
—Robert Frost

23: Epilogue: **Family trees**

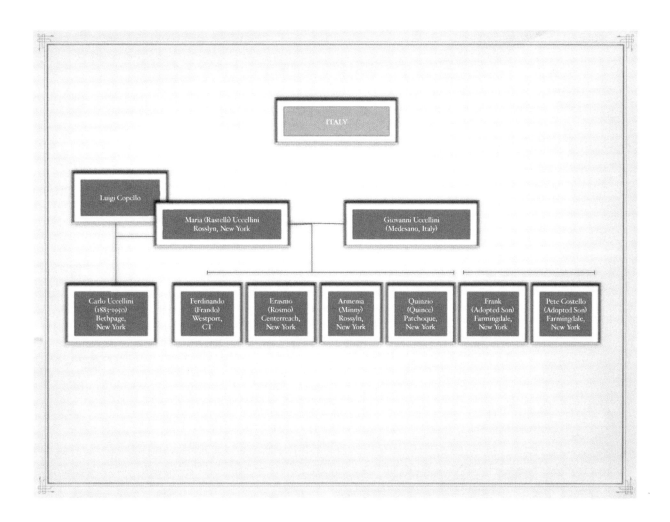

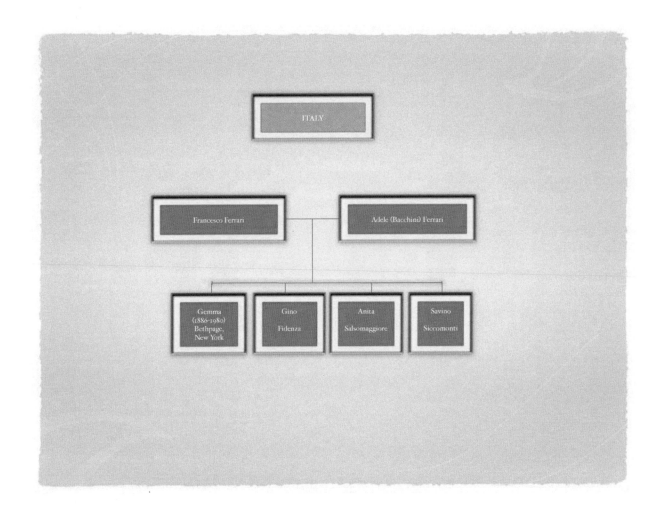

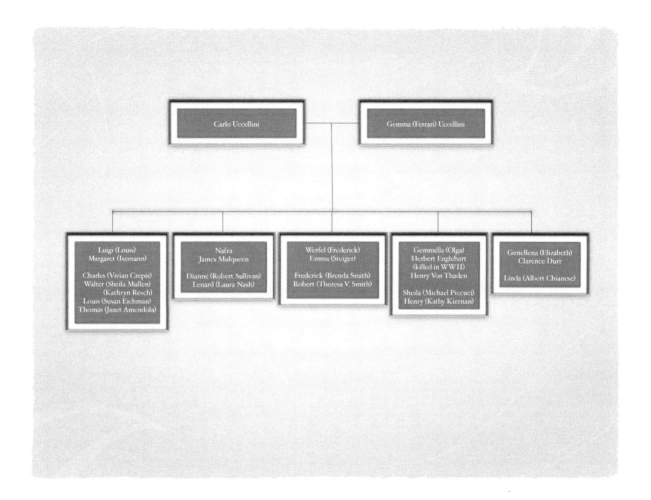

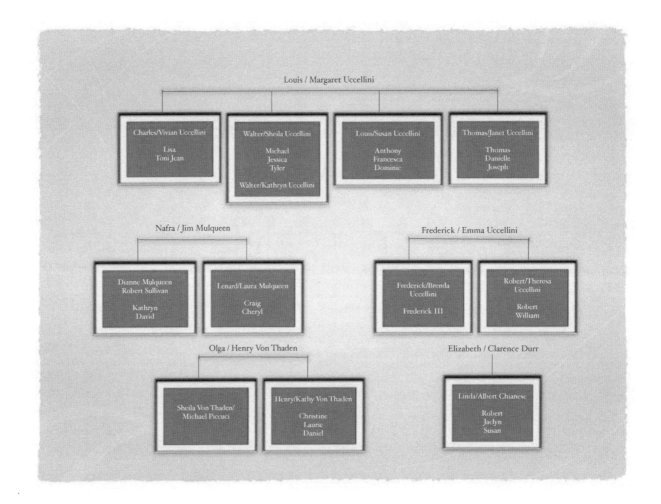

Appendix I: Carlo's Letters to Gemma, 1913

Letter 1.

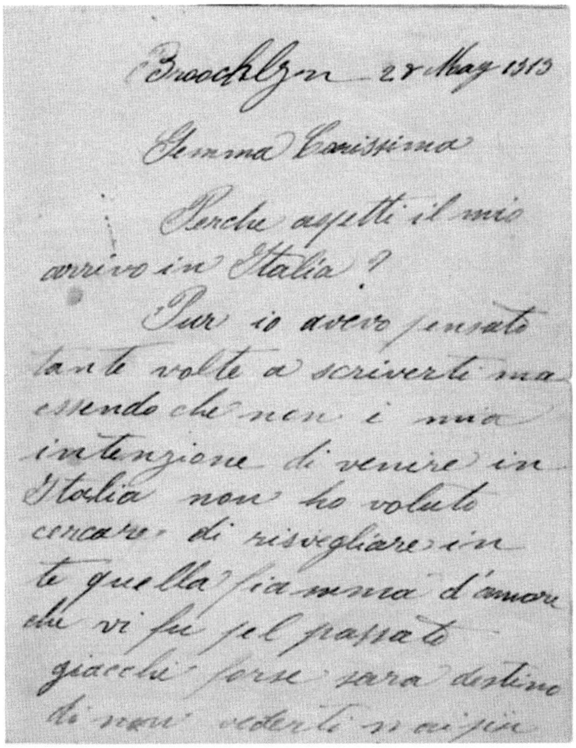

Brooklyn 27 May 1913

Gemma Carissima

Perché aspetti il mio arrivo in Italia?

Pur io avere pensato tante volte a scriverti ma essendo che non è mia intenzione di venire in Italia non ho voluto cercare di risvegliare in te quella fiamma d'amore che vi fu pel passato giacché forse sarà destino di non vederti mai più

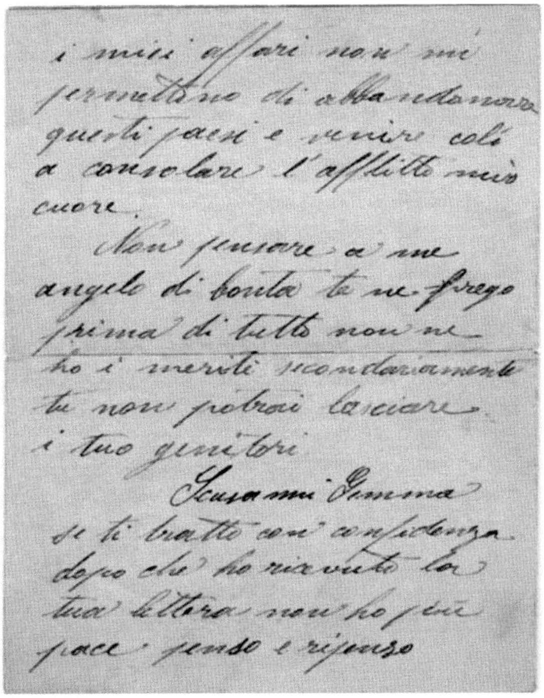

i miei affari non mi permettono di abbandonare questi paesi e venire colà a consolare l'afflitto mio cuore.

Non pensare a me angelo di bontà te ne prego prima di tutto non ne ho i meriti secondariamente tu non potrai lasciare i tuo genitori

Scusami Gemma se ti tratto con confidenza dopo che ho riavuto la tua lettera non ho più pace penso e ripenso

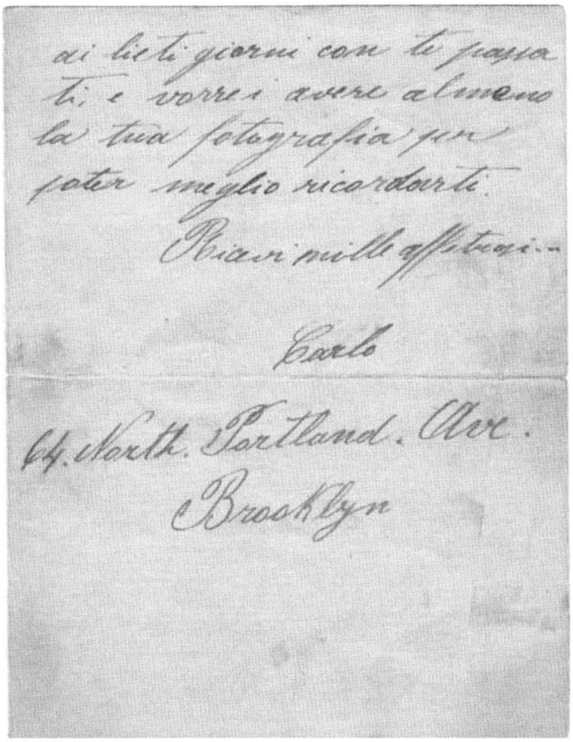

ai lieti giorni con te passati e vorrei avere almeno la tua fotografia per poter meglio ricordarti.

Riavi mille affettuosi...

Carlo

64 North Portland Ave.
Brooklyn

Letter 2.

Brooklyn 8 Luglio 1913

Gemma Carissima

Che significa quel pensiero che mi mandi?

E quello forse il pensiero del tuo cuore?

Sei tu libera ancora

Pensi ancora a me, a quell'uomo che fu così ingrato contro di te

Oppure sono io che nell'estasi beato dei ricordi passati sto sognando un avvenire felice?

Eppoi Gemma mi hai sempre trattato con del tu e così devi fare adesso.

Ricordati di me e rispondi che le tue lettere sono un balsamo per l'animo mio.

Tengo ancora il tuo primo bacio impresso nel mio cuore, e te ne invio uno simile a quello il quale vorrei restare impresso nel tuo

Ti saluto e vorrei averti fra le mie braccia

Parla con confidenza fammi sperare e poi vendicati che lo merito.

Però se un cuore pentito merita perdono, e se tu sei capace di perdonare, fammi sapere se ti piacerebbe venire in America ed abbracciare quell'uomo che ti desidera.

Per ora non ti mando il ritratto perché non l'ho ma quanto prima sarà possibile lo farò fare e soddisfarò il tuo desiderio

per confondere i miei ai baci tuoi

Che il cielo ti benedica

Tuo affmo

Carlo
64 North Portland Ave
Brooklyn. N.J.

Letter 3.

Brooklin 6 Settembre 1913

Gemma Diletta

Col ventitre Agosto ti ho
spedito un altro mio
ma il pensiero che ho verso
di te mi spinge a scriverti
ancora per avere più
presto tue nuove.

Gemma tu non sai
immaginare come sia
grande in me il desi
derio di possederti mai
come ora ho apprezzato
il tuo amore tu sei stata
l'unica che mi sia
rimasta fedele e meriti

la dovuta ricompensa.

Come sarei beato poterti
far mia domani ma
forse la lontananza
ce lo impedisce, tu non
vorrai lasciare le tue terre
il tuo paese natio, per
venire tra le braccia
di chi ti ama in terra
straniera. Ed io non
posso lasciare questa terra
di libertà per venire a
servire un governo che
non mi piace.

Ascolta Gemma
Se è vero che mi ami se
il mio cuore può farti

felice io te lo dono e
tu sii forte abbastanza
da valcare la distanza
che ci separa. Ci sarò
io al porto quando arrivi
ti stenderò le mie braccia
ti farò mia all'istante
se lo desideri.

Fra due settimane
vado in città per restavi
ti manderò la mia foto
grafia e poi se ti de
cidi di venire vieni anche
subito se vuoi, dici a tuo
padre che ti paghi il viaggio
che glie lo rinforsero subito
appena lo sapro, se poi
tuo padre non potesse

scrivimi subito che ci pense
rò io per tutto.

Procurati le mie e
le tue fedi di nascita e poi
vedrai che arriveremo a
godere la felicità che
da tanto tempo affettiamo
Ti bacio tuo affmo
per la vita
Carly
Salutato i tuoi Genitori e
quando la vedi da un bacio
per me a mia Mamma

Letter 4.

Brooklyn 29 Settembre 1913

Tesoro mio

Il tuo eloquente modo di scrivere mi reca piacere immenso. Credo di aver trovato in te la donna che da tanto tempo cerco, ma come poter arrivare a possederti, però se mi comprenderai, se quello che scrivi sarà veramente il sentimento del tuo cuore e la tua volontà sarà di unirti a me e formare la tua famiglia, se rifletterai per bene quello che ti scrivo saprai prendere una decisione.

Io ti amo con tutta la forza dell'animo mio, mai in vita mia ho amato come ora, mai ho compreso la necessità

Io desidero una compagna, il destino volle che incontrassi te, io ti ho scelto, tu sei la preferita, sicché se vuoi essere mia sai come devi fare scrivimi che ti amo il passaggio pagato ed io sarò prontissimo.

Se poi hai timore, se mi credi capace di offenderti, no, ti presto i denari, tu puoi venire in America libera padrona di te stessa, le donne qui trovano lavoro facilmente, anzi sono ricercate. Sicché quando sei qui se non sarai disposta ad essere la mia compagna puoi in poco tempo lavorando guadagnarti i soldi anche per ritornare in Italia, se invece è quello che scrivi sarà la veri-

di amare come ora, ma nel medesimo tempo devo pensare che solo amore non si vive, e questo devi considerarlo tu pure, la ragion che io non voglia venire in Italia per un semplice capriccio, ma invece non è così, considera mia cara, se io venissi in Italia non solo correrei rischio di fare due anni di soldato, ma spenderei dal mio portafoglio mille e cinquanto lire per le spese del viaggio andata e ritorno per me e il tuo, sicché io in Italia non o potrei più restare perché assolutamente non mi piace, dunque se tu mi ami considererai anche il mio interesse che è anche il tuo.

E tu se decidi di essere mia io non ho per te nessuna pretesa, desidero da te amare, fedeltà per l'avvenire, il passato o buono o cattivo io non lo considero per niente poiché non c'è nulla da intendersi, io capisco bene quello che scrivi e se vuoi siamo

ma, sono forte mia moglie, prima che tu scenda dal bastimento così che nulla ne andrebbe del tuo onore, perché non la credo così disonesta andare nelle braccia di colui che t'ama.

Deciditi e via anche troppo che siamo divisi, facciamo che i nostri cuori abbiano libero sfogo fa in modo che possiamo arrivare a godere tutte le delizie che Iddio procura agli amanti fedeli.

Non aspettare più a lungo io ti aspetto.

Ricevi un sincero bacio dal tuo affmo

Carly

Appendix II: Carlo's Patent for Pelt Cleaning and Treating Machine

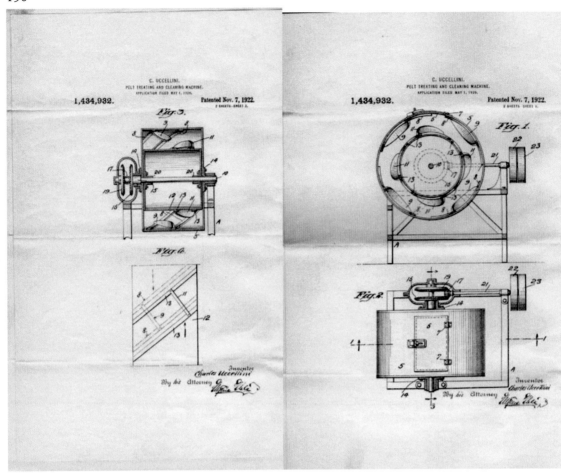

C. UCCELLINI.
PELT TREATING AND CLEANING MACHINE.
APPLICATION FILED MAY 1, 1920.

1,434,932.   Patented Nov. 7, 1922.
2 SHEETS—SHEET 2.

Fig. 3.

Fig. 6.

Inventor
Charles Uccellini
By his Attorney

C. UCCELLINI.
PELT TREATING AND CLEANING MACHINE.
APPLICATION FILED MAY 1, 1920.

1,434,932.   Patented Nov. 7, 1922.
2 SHEETS—SHEET 1.

Fig. 1.

Fig. 2.

Inventor
Charles Uccellini
By his Attorney

Patented Nov. 7, 1922.   1,434,932

UNITED STATES PATENT OFFICE.

CHARLES UCCELLINI, OF CENTRAL PARK, NEW YORK.

PELT TREATING AND CLEANING MACHINE.

Application filed May 1, 1920. Serial No. 378,059.

To all whom it may concern:

Be it known that I, CHARLES UCCELLINI, a subject of the King of Italy, and a resident of Central Park, Nassau County, State of New York, have invented certain new and useful Improvements in Pelt Treating and Cleaning Machines, of which the following is a specification.

My invention relates to machines for treating pelts of animals such as foxes, rabbits, squirrels, skunks, etc., etc., and has for its object a construction whereby the pelts of such animals are more readily and completely cleaned and softened than in prior constructions, and the process or operation of such cleaning and softening is performed at a great saving of time which is now required therefor. To this end I have constructed a mechanism comprising two drums, one drum being relatively rotatable to the other and by means of such relative rotation and the provision of mixing blades and ribs, I obtain a more complete, thorough and intimate mixing of the sawdust which is employed in such drum for rubbing contact with the pelts for softening and cleaning the same. The employment of sawdust for this purpose is well known, the sawdust, and the pelts to be cleaned and softened being ordinarily introduced within a single rotating drum and the sawdust being preferably in a moist condition, the moisture serving to attain more particularly the desired softening effect upon the pelts. The object of my invention, therefore, does not relate to that process, but relates to an improved mechanism for better accomplishing the desired result.

In the accompanying drawings, Fig. 1 is a section taken on line 1—1 of Fig. 2; Fig. 2 is a plan view of Fig. 1; Fig. 3 is a cross-section on line 3—3 of Fig. 2 and Fig. 4 is a diagrammatic view showing the interior arrangement of projecting ribs and intersecting blades or cleats in the inner and outer drums respectively. Having reference to these drawings 5 represents the outer drum of my construction, which drum may be made either of metal or wooden slats and which is provided with the usual door 6 which may be hinged as shown at 7 or otherwise secured upon the drum to give access to the interior of the drum. Upon the inner circumference of this drum 5 I secure a series of ribs 8 preferably diagonally disposed to the axis of the drum and I secure upon these ribs a plurality of projecting blades or cleats 9 extending toward the journal 10, the said cleats being carried by and intersecting the ribs 8 and, in conjunction with the blades or cleats 11, hereinafter described, serving to stir up and thoroughly mix the sawdust placed in the drum.

Within the outer drum and upon the same journal 10 thereof, I mount an inner drum 12, which may be made of any desired material such as metal or wood and provide upon the outer circumference thereof a plurality of diagonally disposed ribs 13 somewhat similar to the diagonal ribs 8, and I secure upon such ribs blades or cleats 11 similar to the blades or cleats 9, the respective cleats projecting toward one another for intimate contact with a softness of mass between, however, for the pelts and sawdust to pass between when the drums are rotated and the cleats or blades pass one another in their opposite rotation. As shown in the drawings, the blades or cleats have their outer surfaces rounded, so as to prevent tearing or otherwise injuring the articles to be treated. The two drums above described are designed to be rotated in opposite directions and for this purpose I have shown in my drawings a sleeve 14 secured upon one side of the outer drum, said sleeve being rigidly mounted upon the collar 15 of the beveled gear 16 which is rotatably mounted upon the journal 10. This beveled gear 16 is engaged by a beveled gear 17 and through the rotation of the latter, rotation is imparted to the gear 16, its collar 15 and the sleeve 14 secured upon the outer drum. For the purpose of rotating the inner drum, I provide a gear 19, similar to the gear 16 but oppositely located thereto and likewise mounted upon the journal 10 and rotated by the rotation of the gear 17. This latter gear 19, however, is fixedly mounted on the journal 10 and rotates the same. By means of sleeves 20, 20 secured upon the inner sides of the inner drum 12 and fixed upon the journal 10, the said inner drum will be rotated, such rotation being in a direction opposite to that of the outer drum 5. The journal 10, the drums, the gears, the gear-box and appurtenant parts are supported on a framework, which I have generally indicated in

the drawings by the reference letter A, and the beveled gear 17 as indicated is rotated by means of a journal 21 carrying the usual loose and fast pulleys 22 and 23 at its outer end.

From the foregoing description it will appear that in my construction of machine for cleaning and softening pelts, I have provided means for securing continuous agitation of the pelts and the sawdust employed in that operation; that the oppositely rotating drums, one within the other, present the adherence by centrifugal force of the contents of the drum to the inner circumference thereof and that my arrangement of ribs and blades intersecting one another in the course of rotation serve to continuously and effectively stir up the mass located between the respective drums.

What I claim and desire to secure by Letters Patent is:

1. In a machine for treating pelts, the combination of an outer rotating drum mounted upon a horizontal axis adapted to receive and confine sawdust and pelts to be treated, ribs secured to the inner circumference of said outer drum, an inner rotating drum, ribs secured upon the outer circumference of said inner drum, the respective ribs being diagonally disposed to the axis of said drums, and mechanism for rotating said drums in opposite directions.

2. In a machine for treating pelts, the combination of an outer rotating drum mounted upon a horizontal axis adapted to receive and confine sawdust and pelts to be treated, ribs secured to the inner circumference of said outer drum, an inner rotating drum, ribs secured upon the outer circumference of said inner drum, the respective ribs being diagonally disposed to the axis of said drums, and extending from one end wall of the respective drum to the other, and mechanism for rotating said drums in opposite directions.

3. In a machine for treating pelts, the combination of an outer rotating drum mounted on a horizontal axis and adapted to receive and confine sawdust and pelts to be treated, diagonally disposed ribs secured upon the inner circumference of said outer drum; diagonally disposed blades secured upon said ribs; an inner rotating drum, diagonally disposed ribs secured upon the outer circumference of said inner drum; diagonally disposed blades secured upon said ribs, both sets of blades having rounded outer surfaces and mechanism for rotating said drums in opposite directions.

CHARLES UCCELLINI.

Appendix III: Gino's letters to Gemma, 1928 and 1938 regarding Gemma's selling of her share of Cantalupo.

Letters from Gino to Gemma. 1928 - 38.

152

Bargoni 28/12/38

Cara Sorella

Da molto tempo che non ricevo
un tuo scritto. Avendo passato le
feste di Natale senza ricevere le
tue notizie sono stata molto
triste. Essendo oggi venuto qui
il fratello Savino per sentire se
avevo ricevuto qualche notizia
da te e qui in tua presenza
ti scriviamo. Noi fratelli stiamo
bene tutti come anche le nostre
famiglie come pure vogliamo
sperare di te e la tua famiglia
e che il silenzio non sia stato causa di

giudizio di premura. Il fratello Savino
ti dice che t'è qui in presenza
a piacere sapere se ài ricevuto
l'ultimo scritto del Dottore di
legge che ancora attende, che doveva
essere firmato dal consolo li
D'America. Che gia di dissi che
non stava bene perché non era
ancora firmato dal consolo
Ti preghiamo e ti supplichiamo
di farci un grosso piacere a
rispondere subito in proposito a
spidire quelle carte che il dottore
à rimandato in dietro da firmare
Mi dirai se ài della spesa per
rimandarmi quelle carte lo dirai
che noi li rimborseremo. Come
ti dico che bisogna che fabricano

trovando la casa puntellata in
pericolo crollezione. Ma prima
di fabricare bisogna che facciano
rogito con noialtre perché l'ufficio
del registro se ci trova il fabricato
nuovo senza che noi abbiamo fatto il
rogito sano in multa Ma non
piccola? In attesa d'un
tuo scritto ti mandiamo tanti
auguri di un buon principio
d'Anno che ti possa l'anno
nuovo portarti qui in Italia
te il marito e figli
Saluti da tutta la mia famiglia
a tutta la tua, tua sorello
Annita e Savino
Ferrari Savino
saluti da tutta la mia
famiglia

Appendix IV: Summary of notes taken during an interview with Perry DeLalio (December 13, 2015)

Interview conducted by Louis W. Uccellini, assisted by Leonard Mulqueen. Perry DeLalio paged through a first edition of the Carlo/Gemma book, as he reminisced about his Italian roots, his growing up/living in Bethpage during the period 1920's into the middle/late portion of the 20th Century, and most importantly his friendship with the Uccellini family and continued respect for Carlo and Gemma and their children. Perry was 93 years old and within 6 weeks of his death when this interview was conducted. He tended to repeat his stories and his memories of Carlo and his boys. His mind was sharp and he lit up when I gave him a copy of the book and he continually looked through it, remembering stories and names as he did so. He and his immediate family were close friends of the Uccellini family and he wanted me to know that he was a close lifelong friend of my father Louis D. Uccellini and that he was delighted to have me (Louis' son) in his home.

1) Perry DeLalio was a close childhood friend of Louis D. Uccellini.

2) Perry's father, Pierro, came from a small town, Cella, just outside of Medesano. Perry emphasized that all of the Italians in Bethpage that came from the Parma area actually came from the area around Medesano. *"Medesano was the heart and soul of this group."* Perry described his father's trip to America: *"he picked himself up from his home, walked several miles to catch a train to the coast (of France) and then embarked on a ship to America, in 1917 (during the war). Pierro's brother (Leonaldo) was already in America, waiting for him"*.

2a) His father (Pierro) married Helen May Appollini in the early 1920's, and they had two children (Pierro, known as "Perry" throughout his life and his sister Lynn). They eventually moved to and developed a farm on Hicksville Road, near Central Ave.

2b) Pierro's brother (Leonaldo) married Emma Appollini (yes, the brothers married sisters) and they had at least 6 boys. They lived near Uncle Frank and Aunt Louisa in Melville (east of Rt. 110). *"Emma did not like living out in the middle of nowhere"* and thus moved to a house on Rt. 109 near William Street in Farmingdale. They lived right around the corner from my mother's (and Aunt Dottie, Aunt Ada and Uncle Louis Isemann) home on 137 William Street. My mother's family knew the DeLalio family before meeting my father. Also should note here that Uncle Frank's wife (Louisa) bitterly complained about living in the Melville farm area right up to her dying day and even complained to me and my wife Susie about the crazy Uccellini's (who made her live out there) when I first introduced Susie to them in the early 1970's. Apparently she wasn't alone with those feelings.

3) Perry knew my father Louis D. Uccellini right from childhood (Perry was 8 1/2 years younger than my father).

4) Basically all the Italians from Medesano were farmers. All of them worked on or operated "truck farms" growing parsnips, lettuce, carrots, potatoes and other produce. All of the produce was delivered to the Brooklyn Market.

5) Perry had tremendous respect for Carlo. *"Carlo was the go-to man for the entire Medesano-based clan of Italians living in that area." "Carlo was a very smart man."* Perry emphasized that point over and over again. *"Carlo could translate anything and everything from Italian to English and English to Italian. People would come to him from the whole region to make sure Italian papers were properly translated to English. Carlo built everything he used. He invented the Carrot Washer and other tools and machines. Everybody brought him things to fix."*

Lenny Mulqueen added that Carlo was a cooper. He made his own wine barrels in the basement and then rolled them up and out through a special double door (that opened out to the driveway) and then rolled them to the barn. Perry added that these barrels were considered the best, tightly fitted-never leaked. Lenny also noted that Carlo made his own wine press. During a phone conversation after this interview, Cousin Fred added that Carlo was a Master Blacksmith, a skill that really added to his skill set for building and fixing everything he worked with.

Back to Perry DeLalio:

6) Most Italian families relied on truck farming to make a living. They often found themselves without enough money to get through the winter. *"But Carlo was different."* He often had side jobs (like maintaining the section of the Old Motor Parkway near Bethpage); and, according to Perry, Carlo operated a still in the barn. *"He made whiskey, good whiskey, very strong whiskey." "He made enough money to carry his family through the winter and more."*

7) Carlo would use the "more", the cash reserve, to lend money to other Italian families that were close friends, money that allowed them to get through the winter. *"Carlo would lend $300 to $400 to his friends on a handshake."* When Perry spoke to this part of Carlo's life, he had a big mischievous smile on his face; but he came back to how important these loans were to the families who received them. This money was essential to them to get through the winter and spring.

8) Perry often came back to my grandfather and how smart he was. *"Carlo could build anything."* Perry then went to my father Louis and his brother Fred: *"They could build anything just like their father Carlo."*

9) Perry focused on the carrot washer as he did in the short note he wrote to the Central Park-Bethpage Historical Society newsletter (see pages 80-82). Perry noted that his father, Pierro, bought the last Carrot Washer Carlo made in the early 1940's as Carlo got noticeably sick with the Parkinson's Disease. *"The Carrot Washer was very effective; load the carrots in the back of the washer and turn the barrel which forced the carrots forward as the water and scraping along the sides cleaned off the dirt which then ran out underneath. Clean vegetables would then come out the front."*

10) The Big News here: The Carrot Washer in the brochure (reproduced on page 82) was the one his father purchased from Carlo; the last one Carlo made. Pierro is in the back, loading the carrots into the Washer. Lorenzo Zarro (recently from Berceto, Italy) is in the front looking directly at the camera. The picture was taken on the DeLalio farm on Hicksville Road, right in front of the new barn they had built as they expanded the farm.

11) Perry lost the top half of his left index finger in the carrot washer, *"fooling around"*. He sheepishly held up his hand to show the top half of his finger was indeed gone.

12) Carlo's hope was that his sons, Louis and Fred, would take over the production of the Carrot Washers. They didn't, as they both got jobs in the growing aircraft manufacturing industry that developed rapidly on Long Island by the early 1940's. Both Fred and Louis gravitated towards work that involved building things. ***"They were both interested in aviation,"*** perhaps the fascination from the Lindbergh flight discussed on page 84.

13) So as Carlo got weaker in the early 1940's from the Parkinson's Disease, he was shaking noticeably; ***"his hands were shaking."*** He would visit the DeLalio farm and his hands would shake more and more. ***"He couldn't build the Carrot Washer and the boys went elsewhere with their building skills."***

14) Perry fondly remembers Fred building the Ferris wheel. He remembers my father helping to build and repair the different farm buildings. But he emphasized several times how both of them built airplanes; Fred at Grumman's and my father at Aircraft Specialty before our entry into, and during, World War II.

15) Perry then focused on my father and how he came into working at Aircraft Specialty. He recalled that a lawyer in Farmingdale named Hogan (who lived on Knob Hill near the Bethpage Golf Course) had a partner named Russell both of whom were friends with the (Emma/Leonaldo) DeLalio family living in Farmingdale. Russell opened up Aircraft Specialty and hired my father before Pearl Harbor and our entry into World War II. My father probably was introduced to Russell through the DeLalio to Hogan link. My father rose up through the ranks very quickly to become the shop foreman because he could design and build the "jigs" needed to mass produce the airplane parts required by Grumman Aircraft, who were themselves spinning up their factory complex in Bethpage to mass produce fighter planes which were eventually to become a major contributor to the Pacific war effort during World War II. Perry was again effusive in his praise for both Louis and Fred as he described how they could build "anything", even when it came to mass producing airplane parts (Louis, a "master builder" of the jigs and the parts themselves) or an airplane itself (Fred; who worked in Grumman before and during the War).

16) Perry then turned to the social interactions. All the Italian friends loved getting together at Carlo and Gemma's house to play cards outdoors (saying they played loudly); to play Bocce (lots of arguments ended when someone would kick the ball away to start the next round). Gene Bellini's name came up as Perry recalled these types of social interactions and noted how close the Bellini family was to Carlo and Gemma and other Italian families around that area.

17) He knew Gene Bellini quite well and they continued to interact when Perry became a successful real estate developer and Gene Bellini ran a successful landscape business from his homestead along Central Avenue near the railroad crossing and Old Motor Parkway. When Gene Bellini moved his landscape business to Dix Hills, he sold his land to Perry who then built the housing development that now sits on the Bellini plot. The road leading into the Bellini development is named *"Parma Avenue"*. Perry said that was his idea *"as a tribute to the home country"*.

18) Perry also knew Woody Lang, another one of the friends from Bethpage who stayed in contact with my father and Nafra through the years. Perry lit up when I brought up Woody's name.

19) Several times Perry would recall Carlo coming to their farm on Hicksville Road when he was getting sick with the Parkinson's disease. Perry simply looked at Lenny and me when he said *"his hands were shaking"*. And Perry would often come back to the whiskey still and laughed about how clever Carlo was (and a good businessman, too).

John Amendola confirmed that the whiskey still existed and that Carlo had run an underground water pipe from the house to the barn. John reemphasized that Carlo converted the still in the early 30's from making whiskey to making fuel for the race cars that were competing on the growing number of race tracks that were becoming increasingly popular on Long Island during that period. John said that the fumes from making the fuel in the barn were really bad, saying that he could not stay in the barn when Carlo was making the fuel because the fumes were so bad. John wondered if this brought on the Parkinson's disease: Besides working in a closed environment when he made the fuel in the barn, John noted, *"He always had his head in the barrels when he cleaned them out."*

20) Perry on his own, and without any prodding, remembered *"that beautiful young girl dying of cancer"*. He just looked out at us and brought this into our conversation. I opened up the Carlo/Gemma book and showed him the Chapter 21 on Sheila. He looked through those pages and said, *"I was very upset, the entire town was upset—she was so beautiful"*.

21) The DeLalio farm (where Perry grew up) on Hicksville Road was gradually converted from growing vegetables to growing flowers and other plants; an enterprise that was well recognized throughout the region. When they sold that farm, they bought the Anderson Green Houses in Farmingdale. Perry moved onto other ventures including real estate and housing development noted above.

22) Perry then came up with a shocker as he casually mentioned that he knew about Carlo's birth story and that he knew about the "Priest Copello in Fornova" (When my father visited Parma in 1985, he met with a priest Luigi Copello who descended from the Copello family and told my father the story as well). Apparently many of Carlo's friends knew of Carlo's birth story.

23) Perry emphasized that the DeLalio family remained good friends with the Uccellini family. Perry remained good friends with my father until my father died in 1989. His mother Helen May and father took Nanny to Florida several years after Grandpa died.

I remember Nanny's trip to Florida, her two-week absence, and then upon her return, how I tattled on my mother and father being mean to me while she was gone. Unlike Nanny, who gave me coffee every morning when I visited her, my parents would not give me coffee while she was gone. I remember that I ended my story by wanting Nanny to spank both of them. Smiles all around, and coffee served the next morning when I walked over to Nanny's house, the routine restored.

24) His Aunt Emma DeLalio (from Farmingdale) is the DeLalio pictured with Gemma on page 124, not his mother Helen May who was much shorter than Emma.

25) As Perry tired (we carried on with this visit and interview for well over an hour and a half), he recounted Italian names which settled on Long Island and in or around the Bethpage area as they all started their new life's journey (John Bellini, George Melvessi, Appollini, Pensorelli...), and then we agreed to stop.

I never did get to ask him about the Lindbergh flight and whether he knew about it (he was rather young; only 4 ½ years old when Lindbergh took off from Roosevelt Field) or whether Carlo and the grownups talked about their experiences with this event unfolding in front of him. I also wanted to ask if he knew anything about the upstate farm. I tried contacting him in early January to follow up on these questions, but received no reply. I then learned from Lenny that Perry DeLalio passed away on February 11, 2016.

**Perry DeLalio and Louis W. Uccellini,
December 13, 2015**

Perry W. DeLalio Sr Obituary
Date of Birth: Tuesday, January 9th, 1923
Date of Death: Thursday, February 11th, 2016
Funeral Home: Brockett Funeral Home
brockettfuneralhome.com
203 Hampton Road
SOUTHAMPTON, New York 11968

Obituary:

Pierre "Perry" W. Delalio Sr. was born on a small farm in Greenlawn, New York to Pierre and Mae Delalio, who farmed trees and vegetable. Their farmhouse burned in 1936 forcing them into Brooklyn, where he graduated from Boys High School in 1941. After graduating, Perry joined his father on the farm and in 1947 married Eileen Brand, a neighboring farmer's daughter. They had two sons, Perry Jr. and Gary. The farm was sold, for development, in 1954. He then went into the nursery business. Perry Sr. became very active in the Farm Bureau and received awards for best chrysanthemums in New York State. For two years running DeLalio chrysanthemums were planted along Park Avenue in New York City. Bethpage Rotary was founded in 1957. Perry Sr. was a charter member and president from 1958-1959. He had 40 years of perfect attendance and, combined with his membership in the Southampton Club, served rotary for over 60 years.

In the early 1960's the nursery was sold and Perry Sr. went into commercial real estate and a poultry farming partnership in Levittown, NY. He also served on numerous boards of the Boy Scouts, and became an active member of the Holy Name Society, Knights of Columbus, and the Bethpage Fire Department Rescue Company. He still received Christmas cards from the children he helped deliver, who couldn't make it to the hospital, from rural Nassau County.

He purchased Southampton Coal & Produce in 1974 and moved permanently to Southampton a few years later. He was a board member of Oil heat Institute. In 1988 Perry Sr. retired from business but stayed very active in Southampton Rotary, Our Lady of the Hamptons RC School and Our Lady of Poland parish council. He was always happy to volunteer for a good cause and could be seen taking tickets at various functions throughout Southampton. In addition, Perry also founded the Zero Club which consists of retired business people meeting for lunch one day a month. The club's motto (no name, no dues and no rules) were testament to the lighthearted conviviality Perry embodied.

His wife, Eileen, died in 2007. Perry Sr. is survived by his sister Lynn Bagli (Frank), his two sons Perry DeLalio Jr. (Sarah) and Gary DeLalio. He is also survived by five grandchildren, Perry DeLalio III (Jen), Elizabeth Sanicola (Joe), Katherine Turza (Brian), Michael DeLalio (Keri), Thomas DeLalio and nine great grandchildren. He would also count numerous close friends among his extended family. His remarkable humor was evident when his sister called to check on him during Superbowl 50 and was told to call back when the game was finished. He will be lovingly remembered by all his Southampton friends for his bright yellow car, with the American flag attached to the antenna, in which he was frequently seen driving around town.

Made in the USA
Middletown, DE
14 December 2020